UNMANAGE

UNMANAGE

NARESH PURUSHOTHAM

Copyright © 2018 Naresh Purushotham

Publishing Services by Happy Self Publishing
www.happyselfpublishing.com

Year: 2018

All rights reserved. No reproduction, transmission or copy of this publication can be made without the written consent of the author in accordance with the provision of the Copyright Acts. Any person doing so will be liable to civil claims and criminal prosecution.

Table of Contents

Foreword by Hal Krause vii

Acknowledgements..xi

Introduction..1

What Inspired This Book?..13

Chapter One: A Brief History of Management 19

Chapter Two: Management in Today's World..........27

Chapter Three: Management in India - Manufacturing 35

Chapter Four: Management in India - Hospitality and the BPO Industry 49

Chapter Five: Management in India - The Indian IT Industry..57

Chapter Six: Management in India - Comparative Analysis... 63

Chapter Seven: The Cultural Implications
of Being a Manager in India 67

Chapter Eight: Management for Today's World 75

Chapter Nine: Integrity 99

Chapter Ten: Trust 107

Chapter Eleven: Credibility 125

Chapter Twelve: Transparency 129

Chapter Thirteen: Motivation 151

Chapter Fourteen: Delegation 163

Chapter Fifteen: Empowerment 181

Chapter Sixteen: The Human Side of Business 183

Afterword 205

Appendix I: Company Case Studies 207

Appendix II: Employee Engagement Survey 251

Appendix II B: Performance Appraisal Survey 257

References 261

A Request 267

Foreword by Hal Krause

> "Nearly all men can stand adversity, but if you want to test a man's character, give him power."
>
> – Abraham Lincoln

In many ways, these deeply insightful words summarize the fundamental dynamic embodied in the word "management." No matter how much it may relate to business and processes, at its core, management is about the dynamic of power. It's about an individual or a group having power over others and this power playing out through unilaterally established structures, systems and practices.

Only recently have thinkers, writers, consultants and business practioners started talking about the evolution and transition of management into real leadership. And if we look at how people and organizations have fared over the years in this power game, and test of character, the results aren't flattering. Across the globe, in every industry and culture, management models have struggled to cope with the real needs of people and organizations.

At Crestcom, the worldwide management training organization I founded in 1987, our key goal has been to enable leaders and managers to empower people with tools and techniques to help them perform better. To help them realize their potential as individuals and as teams, and facilitate a liberalized work culture. Our experience, working with thousands of organizations around the world, has given us a broad view of the flavors of management on every continent. And the struggle has been the same. Leaders are still grappling to find a model that truly works for all the stakehoders in business specially in the VUCA world.

I believe **UnManage** addesses this challenge and presents a refreshingly different view on the subject of management.

I have followed Naresh Purushotham's career from the time he led Crestcom's expansion into India in the 1990s. During the last two decades, Naresh has been involved in the training and development of more than 15,000 Indian managerial leaders. In the process, by providing hands-on training and consulting across a broad spectrum of industries, he has gained unique insights why management teams succeed or fail. The concepts he shares in

UnManage clearly come from deep personal convictions shaped by years of personal hands-on experience.

UnManage fearlessly challenges the status quo, by helping professionals ask themselves tough questions about their management styles and leadership in reshaping the way they mold the culture of their organzations. Naresh's genuine concern for how people are treated (and often mistreated) in the hierarchical and power-driven structures of companies, comes through clearly in the human-centric approach presented in this book.

UnManage begins by tracing the origins of modern management practices. While his message applies to managerial leaders worldwide, the emphasis on the Indian context makes the book's message much more immediate and relevant to the Indian business professional.

Naresh stresses that culture and values are central to the success of any managerial leader or team. He powerfully channels Peter Drucker's infamous warning: "Culture eats Strategy for Breakfast."

It is obvious that, after many years working closely with top management teams, he has seen too many organizations fail to get it right by over-focusing on strategic and financial goals while forgetting what it takes to to achieve them. ***UnManage*** urges leaders to focus on three core values—Integrity, Trust, and Crediblity. Values often discussed, but seldom effectively implemented. The book affirms that when leadership concentrates on these values, people feel enabled, empowered, and motivated. Organizations that are successfully weaving these values into the fiber of their business **win**. Those who don't, **lose**.

It is not surprising that the closing message of the book urges readers to reflect on the human side of business and warns management leaders that those who get the people element wrong will never realize optimum growth, purpose, or fruition.

UnManage is well researched, with relevant case studies, reflective exercises, and a management approach that is simple yet truly aspirational.

Written in simple language, the book is an easy, non-pretentious read, which provides a fresh look on how to foster key impactful values and principles!

Hats off, Naresh, on your first book! Thousands of managers, worldwide will benefit immensely from your experience and the practical insights you share in **UnManage**!

Hal A. Krause
Founder, Crestcom International, Ltd

Acknowledgements

To Hal Krause, the founder of Crestcom International and to Crestcom International, who provided me with the know-how to enter the field of learning and development.

To all the Bulletproof Managers and our clients over the last twenty plus years who have reposed faith in us. All that I have learned and shared in this book come from my participants and our engaging sessions over the years.

To Prabodh Sirur for literally goading me to write this book and providing me with his team's support to collate material and even draft the initial chapters—Pankaj Dixit, Lizzie Lewis, Ameya Vijay Potdar, and other team members from Logica (now CGI).

To my colleagues at Crestpoint and my co-founder Lakshmi Vasan who repeatedly reaffirmed that I should also write and not just talk!

To my editor, Sharath Komanraju, who helped me sort out the initial manuscript and gave it the appearance of a book!

To Punctuate Consulting, run by Ambujam Hariharan and Priya Veeraraghavan, for conducting the market research on the associated topics covered in the book.

To Sudha Hariharan who helped research the various case studies for the book.

To the entire team at Crestpoint led by Konrad Fernandez who gave me the motivation for the last mile and Ishwarya Kumar for extracting valuable data from our *Learning 360* surveys administered over the years and for the cherished insights gleaned from them.

I would like to thank Arun Kumar, the cartoonist, for all the sketches that you will find in the book. He has truly captured, light-heartedly, what people have experienced in real life.

To my family—my wife, Menaka, and my daughters, Sahana and Sriranjani—for allowing me to go after crazy pursuits and patiently being part of the roller coaster ride I have taken them on!

To my Dad, he would be proud of the fact that I made something out of my life!

Introduction

We live in an age of information and content. You can find a book (and sometimes a whole shelf of books) on any topic at your friendly neighborhood bookstore or library. If getting out of your house and taking a walk is not your preference, there is information available online as well.

There are blogs and websites. There is Wikipedia and Google. Perhaps for the first time in human history, there is no excuse for saying "I don't have the necessary information."

Management is no different.

CEOs of Fortune 500 companies have written books. Billionaires are interviewed on TV all the time and are asked about their secrets. Coaches of great athletes, captains of great teams, revolutionary leaders—lives of these people are often pored over with a microscope in the hope that the common people will be able to find that one successful mantra that distinguishes great leadership, great management and great teams.

I will tell you right now, though I suspect you know it already. No such mantra exists. If it were possible to make a list of *7 Habits of Successful Managers*, and if those habits had been easy to imbibe into our daily lives, we'd all be successful. We'd all be great. But we aren't. Why?

Because it takes more than knowing what to do. It takes more than blindly following a theoretical model that has been handed down by the bosses. It takes more than inserting an inspirational quote into your email signature.

In the age of information, it is not the person with the most information that wins; but the person who knows what the information means, and what he can do with it. In a study of geniuses taken from different fields—Albert Einstein, Mark Twain, Bill Gates, Ramanujam and Steve Jobs—this is the one trait they were found to share, across generations and centuries and professions. Knowledge is not as important as *knowledge about knowledge*. (Psychologists call this *metacognition*.) Learning is not as important as *learning to learn*.

As our culture becomes more informed and as knowledge becomes ubiquitous, the demand for metacognitive people will only rise. We will need this deeper sense of knowledge in our doctors, our artists, our authors, our politicians, and our managers.

The first aim of this book is to go beyond the values that most other management books talk about, and attempt to understand the core nature and the purpose. For instance, most materials that you've read about management before, would have asked you to become more trustworthy and would have given you some steps to focus on what it is that prevents us from being trustworthy when the stakes are high. In this book, we'll also discuss ways in which we can mitigate this natural behavior to the best of our abilities.

The other purpose of this book is to look deeper at the management through the prism of the Indian cultural milieu. Most management practices and models that corporate India follows today has come from the West (and from Japan), so they fit into the *Indian way of life* much like a square peg into a round hole.

But they're forced to fit because we've been told that they work and that they have worked in organizations where they've been tried before. So we get on top of the square peg and drive it down into the round hole with all the frantic power we can muster. Then, when things don't work out, we wonder why.

In my experience, I've met many people who run organizations based on a checklist that they've read about in Harvard Business Review. If it's good enough for Harvard, they say, it's good enough for us.

The question to be raised is not whether it is *good* enough. The question is whether a model of management designed for a particular culture, will work unchanged when introduced into a different culture. India has a long history and a unique culture. We do things differently here. Our people tick to a different clock.

So shouldn't our management approaches and models be customized?

In any social scenario overseas, asking about somebody's marital or familial status is considered rude. But in India, questions like "what do you do?" and "what does your father do?" are acceptable conversation starters. Just the other day, a woman who lived in the United States paid us a visit. On the walk down the corridor of our office, a colleague asked her if she was married. And she said, "Boy, you guys like to ask personal questions, don't you?"

She had evidently been asked the same question numerous times ever since she landed in the country. I had to explain, rather shame-facedly, that we mean no harm and that asking someone if they are married was not considered impolite according to Indian social customs.

When there is such a glaring social and cultural difference between the West and the East, does it not make sense that the Indian management system should take into account Indian values and sensibilities? Shouldn't our work styles make allowances for the Indian mind? Shouldn't we be examining the models we inherit from the West with a certain amount of skepticism, and shouldn't we look to mold them into a form that is easily digestible to the Indian palette?

My answers are yes, yes, and yes. And in the course of this book, I hope to convince you as well.

The third goal of this book is to introduce a holistic view of management. Very often, we get lost in metrics and platitudes so much that we forget that we are dealing with human beings and that we have to handle intangible, indefinable concepts such as joy, meaning, sacrifice, patience, love and duty that drive people. Metrics are a great way of measuring performance, but I'm yet to meet a number that could make a person give her best.

Human beings are driven not by numerical targets, but by abstractions such as happiness and contentment. So a manager who focuses exclusively on revenue and utilization targets is bound to miss the wood for the trees.

Like everything else, management doesn't sit in a vacuum. A good manager must be a good human being, a trusted friend, and a respected colleague. Your journey to becoming a better manager will also take you on a path to self-discovery and mastery. The better you know yourself, the better you will manage your team.

In short, there are no short cuts. This book will look at management as an extension of being a person, and will invite you to develop a style of management that emerges naturally from your culture, character, and personality. There is no one size, which fits all feet. If you're introverted by nature, you will gain a little by trying to be more assertive and open. If you're extroverted, you will struggle if I advise you to start writing notes to your employees. However, no matter what your personality is, it is possible to devise an effective management style that will work for both you and your teams.

For this, we have to know ourselves.

So I will urge you at this moment to steel yourself, because looking in the mirror can be a little unnerving. If you flinch at certain parts of this book, that's all right. We all have demons of our own to fight, and we must fight them in our little ways. I hope that in the course of this book, you and I will see our respective reflections in the mirror. I hope that we gather the courage to look at our images in the eye. I hope that we take the necessary steps to better ourselves, so that we may become better people and therefore, better managers.

A Structural Overview of the Book

We can think of this book in four parts.

1. A commentary on management – both in India and overseas

    The first two chapters, *A history of Management* and *Management in India*, talk about the foundation of the current system of corporate management that we currently follow. The management structure today reminds one uncannily of the military and the Industrial Revolution eras where strategies were motivated by *command and control* philosophies and a rigid pecking order was necessary to establish order. Back then, there was a sharp demarcating line between thinkers and doers, the strategists and the plebs, which demanded a linear structure of management, where everyone had a superior.

In India, we will look at the history of management through the prism of four different industries: Manufacturing, Information Technology, Hospitality, and BPOs. We will do a comparative analysis of the four industries, and dwell for a while on the cultural implications of being a manager in India, the social status one derives from gaining that title, possible reasons for our thinking being this way, and how we can break out of it.

By the end of this section, the conclusion we will draw is that India is grappling with a dying model, and that we need a better paradigm under which both the managers and the managed thrive without mutual discord.

2. A recommendation of a new management approach

In Chapter 3, I propose a new approach or a more commonsensical one for management effectiveness. This is a triangular structure with three key dimensions—***relationships, tasks, and results***—sitting on two fundamental core values of trust and credibility.

Without trust and credibility, a manager cannot command the respect of his team.

This is the reason our effectiveness model focuses on these two values as absolute cornerstones. The three dimensions are focus areas that every manager should keep an eye on—relationships between himself and his team (and between the team members themselves), tasks that have to be completed in order to achieve the team's goal, and results that the team can achieve.

While results are what every team in the real world is judged by, we will look at ways to minimize the focus on results alone during the process and use relationships and tasks as means to achieve the results that we want.

3. An analysis of various attributes that make up the model

    Through chapters 4 through 7, we will look at how we can use trust and credibility to achieve three other aspects every manager must work on—**transparency, motivation, and empowerment.** We will consider these aspects as *secondary attributes* because they will arise as a consequence of creating and nurturing a team culture based on trust and credibility.

So trust and credibility are the primary attributes. Transparency, motivation, and empowerment are secondary attributes.

This section will contain some interesting anecdotes and case studies that will help us get over our own character gaps and improve ourselves not only to become a better manager but also a better person. The focus is on becoming more trustworthy and credible in our human interactions and relationships.

4. A tribute to values and ethics over profit and revenue

    We will wrap this book up with a discussion on the intangible versus the tangible, the material versus the spiritual. While I do not intend to deliver discourses (like in my sessions!) on how the material world is fleeting and illusory, I do intend to put forward a style of thinking about business and management that is not rooted just in numbers and metrics.

In Chapters 8 and 9, we will discuss ways to align our businesses so that they become more personalized and meaningful. The current trend is to think of numbers and metrics as supreme. Quarterly revenue results are everything. We live and die by our P&L reports. We swear by the balance sheet, while there is just no balance in our lives and relationships.

They're all important, no doubt. But when the numbers and metrics become everything, a danger creeps into our processes, a danger which may lure us into dehumanizing our employees, and looking at them as just a resource instead of a person.

I will close with arguments—aided by case studies and real-life examples of course—that show that if one runs a human business that is trustworthy and credible, empowerment happens on its own. In addition, an empowered corporation is almost always a happy, profitable corporation.

So come right in. Let's talk about how we can **Unmanage** to manage better in a VUCA world.

What Inspired This Book?

Over the last twenty-five years, Crestpoint Consultants Pvt. Ltd., the organization that I co-founded along with Lakshmi Kruti Vasan, has delivered Crestcom's Bullet Proof Manager program to over twenty thousand managers in India. As part of this year long program, we administer a pre and post assessment to measure each participant's before and after progression. We created an instrument called the **Learning 360** that focuses on core behavioral competencies. We called it the Learning 360 because it aids the learner in building an individual development plan (IDP) or a MyDP, as we call it, and is not meant to be an appraisal. Because of its non-threatening nature, our experience is that participants and their raters have openly shared honest and realistic feedback on their managers. Moreover, because it is a 360 approach, we have an all-round view of the manager—from above, below, peer, as well as self.

We have studied the findings from over five thousand such administrations across twenty-four competencies and the insights are fascinating.

This book is an attempt to understand the role of a Manager, the people who move into this role and the fast changing contours of this role. Depending on who dons the role, he or she can become a manager or a damager!

Here are some of the key findings:

1. Delegation – Direct reports have consistently rated their managers low on this competency and managers have predictably rated themselves high on this. This simply means that Indian managers hesitate to delegate and team members are hungry for the challenges. (This is discussed at length in Chapter 7, which addresses delegation.)
2. Motivation – A similar trend where managers rate themselves as high motivators and team members have consistently rated them low on the scale. Somewhere in the Indian psyche, there is this feeling that praising people too much may go to their heads. Comments I have heard in sessions are like this: "Isn't it their job?" "What are we paying them for?" "The moment I praise them, they ask for a raise!"

3. Strategic Thinking/Planning – One area where there seems to be a consensus is strategic planning. It is generally rated low across all levels. Indian managers are aware that they are more tactical and operational, rather than strategic. They also realize that in order to become global leaders they need to become more strategic.
4. Conflict handling – Team members have rated their managers low, while the self-ratings are high. The reality is that managers tend to avoid conflict and typically have a tendency to brush things under the carpet or avoid handling it all together until it blows up. Very few managers use conflict constructively.
5. Communication – Every manager assumes that he or she is good at it! The reality is exactly the opposite. In my experience, I have found that the skill of communication is sorely missing. Very often, this lack of communication effectiveness comes back to haunt them when they get closer to the corner office. I recall an assignment where the organization identified a potential candidate for elevation and the only thing that stood between the person and the top position was the candidate's poor communication style! I was called to coach the person on basic communication skills!

6. Negotiation – Most managers assume that they are very good negotiators until they face their counterparts from the West or Japan. In my experience, most Indian managers are *cowboy negotiators.* They just turn up and start *shooting from the hip.* No preparation, no homework, no planning. And they pay the price—bad deals, lower margins, unrealistic timelines. I could go on.
7. Emotional Intelligence – Managers scored low on this dimension. This surprised me because as a people, we are relationship oriented. In our homes and in our social settings we seem to be emotionally intelligent. When it comes to the office, managers come through as task oriented, transactional, and lacking in sensitivity. In my experience, I find that most managers grapple with this and don't seem to understand the importance of EQ in leading and developing people.
8. Performance Management – Uniformly rated low by team members and borne out amply by our research study on **performance appraisal** presented in the book. Managers generally shy away from creating accountability for results and most appraisals suffer from a lot of subjectivity. As a result, team members are demotivated and managers end up externalizing their

failure, citing the reasons to be normalization, bell curve, etc., and walking away from their core responsibility of assessing performance and standing up for meritocracy.

Competencies assessed in our L360 assessments

(Ranked from least asked to most asked)

Performance management
Raising Productivity
Influence
Conflict Resolution
Innovation
Change management
Emotional Intelligence
Strategic thinking
Time management
Communication
Developing People
Negotiation
Problem Solving
Motivation
Performance Appraisal
Delegation
Leadership
Personal Excellence
Team Building / Team work / Collaboration
Planning
Business Acumen
Customer Centricity
Result Orientation
Accountability

Most corporates ask for an intervention in terms of competencies in the following order (least asked to most asked competencies)

Innovation
Performance management
Accountability
Performance Appraisal
Business Acumen
Developing People
Raising Productivity
Influence
Emotional Intelligence
Planning
Result Orientation
Personal Excellence
Delegation
Motivation
Problem Solving
Leadership
Conflict Resolution
Time management
Team Building / Team work / Collaboration
Strategic thinking
Customer Centricity
Change management
Communication
Negotiation

CHAPTER ONE

A Brief History of Management

The true history of management is impossible to trace. But we can surmise that ever since human beings began to learn the art of speaking to one another within social groups; ever since they banded together to go on hunting and gathering expeditions as teams, a crude form of management must have developed.

If a team of early human hunters were about to set forth into the plains to bring down a bison or a woolly mammoth, they would have first elected a leader. This leader would then decide upon a strategy. He would allocate roles to his team members. His aim would be to ensure that they bring back the mammoth with minimum casualties.

Back at the settlement, the womenfolk would come together in a team, and one or more leaders would take the ownership of guiding the others in their tasks whether that was housekeeping, caring for children, cooking, or gathering material for the evening's bonfire.

> "Ninety percent of what we call management consists of making it difficult for people to get things done."
>
> Peter F. Drucker

So as long as groups and teams have been in existence, they've used some form of management in order to perform their tasks with the most efficiency and the least risk.

Like any word that is commonly used, there is no universally accepted definition for the word **management**. It's a bit like success or happiness. While we may know what we mean when we say these words, no two people ever agree upon their definitions, and too often, many arguments begin and conclude without ever touching upon the meaning of these concepts.

In its most general form management is the art of allowing a team to achieve its objective in the most efficient way possible. This efficiency applies not just to resources in general, but to time and money in particular. In general, the goal of good management is to help the team reach its goal with minimal expenditure of two key resources:

1. Time
2. Money

The question on most managers' lips during the course of the project is two-pronged.

First: Is it on schedule? Second: Is it under budget? At different key points, we will ask ourselves the questions: How will this help me deliver my project on time? How will it help me deliver my project under budget?

On the other hand, more specific definitions of management also exist, but they differ from each other depending on which sector or industry we approach. A military officer's definition of management may be more ruthless, compared to that of a family-owned bakery. A corporate hospital will be run on entirely different management philosophies and targets, than a hotel.

To better understand the evolution of the current-day management in big corporations around the world, let's look at three distinct periods of time.

Management in the Pre-Industrial Revolution Era

For most of human history, management was confined to the army.

The only place where large groups of human beings got together and worked toward a common goal was on the battlefield. Yes, people did gather to work on the fields and in market squares, but they didn't have to be actively managed, mainly because the tools of most trades were mechanical, and were designed to be used by one person at a time.

In the battlefield, though, things were a little different. The general had to marshal his troops, plot and implement strategy, motivate his soldiers, guide them, cajole them, and deploy them at the right moments. On top of this all, he had to be a good fighter himself, because otherwise he could find himself at the wrong end of the opposing general's lance.

It is not an exaggeration to say that in armies, a leader's management skill often is a matter of life and death. In such a high-stakes game, a rigid pecking order and hierarchy were necessary. Orders were meant to be followed come what may because a moment lost in dithering or debate could mean the crucial difference between defeat and victory, life and death.

Management in the army has changed little from the years of Napoleon and Alexander. The weapons of choice have changed, but the structure remains, because the stakes are just as high as they were back then. Kingdoms were smaller then, perhaps, compared to the size of countries we have today, but that only meant that the size of the average army has increased. And so has the sophistry of its strategies, operations, and equipment.

The two Cs of army style management **are command and control**. Frederick the Great, who reigned over the kingdom of Prussia from 1740 to 1786, once said, "Soldiers should fear their officers more than all the dangers to which they are exposed. Good will can never induce the common soldier to stand up to such dangers. He will do so only out of fear."

At another time, he stated, "If my soldiers were to begin to think, not one of them will remain in the army."

In those two quotes, we find the two fundamental tenets upon which management in the army rests: fear of the superior, and the forced sublimation of free thought.

An example may serve to stress why this form of management is preferred in the army. Generally, soldiers are trained to freeze in a minefield. One of the basic army training goals is to embed into soldiers this habit of *freezing* when they find themselves in a location infested with mines. It is not uncommon for army instructors every once in a while to shout "Mine!" in the middle of other activities so that the soldiers would develop a reflex reaction to the word.

Now, the other bit of training that soldiers are put through concerns a situation in which they're under fire. In these cases, they're taught to advance toward their attackers while shooting. The rationale here again is simple—shooting will force your attackers to take cover, and by running toward them, you're getting closer with each step, which makes your aim surer.

What happens when you find yourself in a minefield *and* you're being fired upon? Staying still will make you a sitting duck, and running will put you under risk of being blown up by a mine. What do you do?

The right answer is that you run toward the attackers while returning fire, because that way, at least some of you will survive. Yes, some of you will be taken out by the mines, but you will at least be nullifying the bigger threat: live enemy attackers who can see you and aim.

But ironically, the best solution for the team may not be the best solution for an individual. When everyone else is running toward the attackers, your safest bet as an individual is to freeze, because that way the mines won't get you, and since your live enemy is engaging with the advancing soldiers, you're safe from the live fire too.

So a *thinking* soldier will not advance in such a situation. However, for the best chance of success of the team, he has to advance, and put his life at risk. And to do that, it is important for him not to think. He has to follow orders above everything.

The Industrial Revolution

When the Industrial Revolution came along, the structure of a typical corporation was much like that of an army barracks. There was *the room upstairs*, and there was the *shop floor*. In the room upstairs sat the managers, owners, employers. On the shop floor worked the labor class. The managers sat in plush chairs, smoked cigars, and threw their heads back when they laughed. The workers sweated it out, and waited until the end of the day in a long line, hats in hand, for their wages.

The people upstairs were the thinkers of these companies. They owned the equipment and the land. Every month or so, they went out of town for meetings with politicians and the other bigwigs. They brought back work for their shop floors.

As long as work kept coming in, the doers were happy. As long as the doers stood obediently with their hats in hand, the thinkers were happy.

There was a definite boss. There was a definite subordinate. Hierarchy existed among the managers and the labor classes too, but a man in one stream would rarely cross over to the other.

Like a marriage in the patriarchal society, the demarcation of roles was sharp and well defined. It worked well because it was in the interest of the managers to keep their employees in the dark and on a leash, and it was in the interest of the employee—especially in tough economic conditions—to keep his voice low and his gaze averted.

CHAPTER TWO

Management in Today's World

The internet has democratized the way we do business. With the emergence of Google and then Facebook and Twitter, organizations have tapped into the *social* way of doing things. And what is the primary symptom of being social? It is that every voice is equal, that every voice counts.

New, successful companies are emerging every day that scoff at management structures and hierarchies. There is no line between a thinker and a doer now. Everyone is a thinker, and everyone is a doer.

There are a few reasons for this, the first and most important of which is the fact that businesses have become extremely mechanized now. People on the shop floor no longer need to get their hands dirty and fiddle around with greasy trinkets. However, they do need to know how to work on a computer, how to fire up Microsoft PowerPoint and dash out a presentation at short notice.

So the equity of the world has moved from muscle to mind. This has reduced the gap between the thinkers and doers, and rightly so.

The other reason for this big shift is that in the information era, the correlation between a person's age and his knowledge is breaking down. Until the last decade, an experienced employee almost always knew more than a greenhorn. However, today, all knowledge is available to anyone who knows how to ask the right questions. And the young people, who grew up with Google, know how to find information better, faster, and with more efficiency than members of the older generation who spent much of their lives in the brick and mortar age.

The third reason is that jobs today are extremely specialized. No manager can be expected to know everything within his domain now. Every leader is bound to have team members under him who know more than he does, who have spent more time working at the product in question for longer than he has. The need to listen, to collaborate, and to cooperate has never been higher.

Management across the World: A Comparative Study

In this sub-section, we will look at three different management and work models that are prevalent across the world today.

- Western Work Style
- Japanese Work Style
- Indian Work Style

Western Work Style

- Organizations are run by transactional professional managers with the focus on short-term quarterly results
- Emphasis is on individual responsibility—individualism—highly task oriented and result focused
- Adopt a contractual culture – *"We have a job to do"*
- Clear professional – personal divide in relationships
- Intense market pressure for companies to compete in emerging markets
- High emphasis on training and skills building to cope with the changing context

Japanese Work Style

- Information flow is bottom to top
- Management by consensus
- Manager needs to provide the environment for the team to flourish, be accessible at all times
- Manager seen as a father figure who receives loyalty and obedience from colleagues
- Company strives to provide high quality output while reducing costs/wastage
- Fairness and honesty in all business dealings and personal conduct
- Courtesy and humility
- Loyalty to the firm
- High job security with seniority based compensation
- Close knit – insular and parochial

Indian Work Style

- Hierarchical society, hierarchical work culture
- Manager expects deferential treatment
- Willing to persistently improvise creative solutions, which is known as *jugaad* in India
- Downside to *jugaad* – compromised quality
- Strong cliques between managers, peers, and subordinates

- Loyalty and compliance is high in the Indian work force
- Status and position in society is an important factor
- Work force motivated by individual and silo achievement
- Delegation style is specific to each manager
- Fluid orientation to timelines and fuzzy expectations

Dimensions	US	Japanese	Indian
Relationship	Contractual Formal Professional – personal distance Loyalty to profession	Company Team Pride	Informal Personal + Professional overlap Loyalty to individual/team
Process	Invention	Innovation	*Jugaad*
Results	Short term	Long term	Focus is on individual tasks, rather than results

Since the focus of this book is the Indian management scenario, let's look at how Indian management has had influences from different socio-cultural systems. The diagram below reflects that, and we will discuss it in more detail in coming chapters.

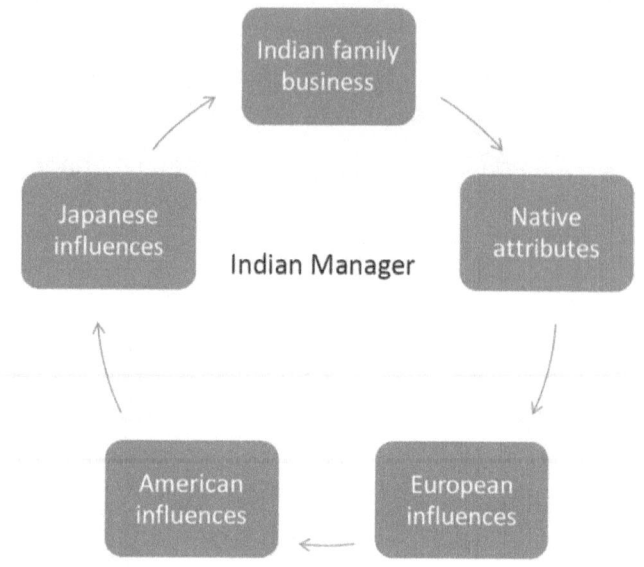

Corporate Life on the Information Highway

There is only one possible conclusion that we can draw from our basic history lesson: old style management is dying. There is a sharp need for a change in the management structures that were imported from the Industrial era. They need to be demolished so that they can be re-built to suit life and needs on the Information Highway.

More specifically, management in India needs a much deeper change, because as we will see, management is an entirely different beast in our country. Owing to our colonial and patriarchal roots, corporate management is a microcosm of Indian society, and if we are to bring processes that are more efficient into our businesses, we must also bring freshness and change into our lives.

In the next chapter, we will take a closer look at a brief history of management from the Indian context.

CHAPTER THREE

Management in India – Manufacturing

Colonial Hangover

At a recent family gathering, the parents of a young man I know were distributing sweets to everyone present. We knew that it was not their son's birthday. It was not their wedding anniversary. There had been—as far as we could tell—no big events shaping up in their lives. After a bit of silence, someone asked the mother what the occasion was.

And she said, beaming proudly as only a mother could, "My son has become a manager."

We congratulated the young man on his *achievement*, but it left me in a maze of thought. The word manager comes with many connotations in India. A manager is a superior, a boss, someone who orders people around and gets work done. He's the thinker who sits on the top floor in his own cabin, while his minions slave away in a pool of sweat on the shop floor.

There must be cultural reasons for this. Because our society is hierarchical, we assume the same structures at our workplaces, and therefore being on the bottom rung is no good, whereas climbing the stairs to the level above you is an achievement, worthy of celebration and appreciation.

We will look at this phenomenon a little more deeply during the course of this chapter. However, to understand the kind of management we do in India, I think it will be helpful to look at the history across various sectors and how the styles differ from one industry to the next.

Manufacturing

Nikolai Kondratieff, a Russian economist, said in the 1920s that the Industrial Revolution in different parts of the world could be visualized as waves. 18th century England started the first wave by focusing on steam engines, textiles, and printing. America in the 19th century picked it up and started the second wave, boosting the automobile sector. Finally, in the 20th century, Japan, with its fervent passion for electronics and automation, created the third wave.

Let's look briefly at each of these waves, and how they affected the evolution of manufacturing in India.

First Wave

In Western civilization, after the discovery of fire, then agriculture, the Industrial Revolution of 18th Century Europe altered human history and culture. It started in Britain—which was the wealthiest nation of the world—and then spread to other nations in the world like Germany, France, and America.

The CBD (Central Business District) became a common household term during this time, because having production houses in close proximity to one another, greatly enhanced efficiency. Cities grew. People moved from villages in search of a better life.

Though the earliest inventions were limited to the textile industry, James Watt invented the steam engine and then applied it to every sector he could see. Wherever goods had to be lifted or moved, the steam engine was present. New fuels such as petroleum and coal began their lives, and as we can see in our present-day world, they're still influencing countless millions of lives.

It was during the first wave of the Industrial Revolution that a *subsistence economy* became a *surplus economy*.

Britain began to produce much more than they needed, and set up trade routes to other countries to earn wealth from their excess goods. They monopolized trade with America—almost half of all British exports in the 1780s went to America—and later with India.

Second Wave

It was during the second wave of the Revolution, in 19th century America, that the corporation was born.

America was the new land of opportunity. The government set up a structure of free markets, and offered land and other financial incentives for entrepreneurs, to lure them into setting up manufacturing hubs. Samuel Slater, often hailed as the father of the American Industrial Revolution, and Du Pont, a Frenchman who established the country's first successful chemical company, both came to America as a response to the enormous financial rewards.

If the first wave was about shifting manufacturing activities from small individual workshops to large factories, the second wave focused on speeding up production and getting the products into customers' hands more quickly than before. Henry Ford created the moving assembly line, where employees stood at one place and parts moved from one to the next, being built a little at each stop, until a finished product emerged at the end.

This was also the time when assembly and specialization gained a feverish pace. Any product now had more components than before, and each component could be designed and manufactured at the same time before they were all brought together to be assembled.

All of these processes—the assembly line, the focus on specialization and parallel performance, and the general increase in size of a company—resulted in the birth of corporations.

And with the birth of corporations came a renewed need for good managers.

Third Wave

The third wave of the Industrial Revolution saw an unlikely Asian participant challenge—and in some ways overtook—the dominion of Britain and America. This started in the electronics industry and then spread to automation. Though these sectors were first set up in Europe and America, Japan revolutionized them and ran to the head of the line.

The foundations of the first two waves were in the materials, resources, and manpower. But in electronics, the focus shifted toward knowledge and intellect. The industry was less prone to monopoly controls and political restrictions. In addition, since it was based on mental ability, it demanded a flatter organizational structure, and the role of the manager changed subtly.

Japan started producing music organs, watches, calculators, numerical controllers for machines, robots and other electronic equipment at such a startling speed. By the mid-1970s, their output was second to the United States.

By 1980, Japan employed around 70 percent of the world's total robot population in their own factories.

The one factor that helped Japan win this battle was the commitment to technology-driven innovation over process-driven innovation. All Japanese electronics companies jostled fiercely with one another in the highly crowded market for consumer goods, and the high R&D budgets, paid rich dividends by raising the quality of automation and efficiency of the produce across the whole industry.

The second factor that helped was the government-industry cooperation. The Japanese government bought into the importance of research and technology driving the next leg of growth. They helped corporations by speeding up grants and funding, setting up protection policies for research centers, and also conducted public funded research to help corporations keep to their growth curves.

Manufacturing in India

The earliest evidence for manufacturing activities in India is present in the ruins of the Harappan Civilization (4000–3000 BC). Studies of life in the Indus Valley have revealed that accurate weights and measures were in use. Kilns were present to smelt copper and to cast tools. There were metal tools in existence, like circular saws and pierced needles. Construction of monuments was a key activity in those times, so technologies for lifting, loading, transportation, and scaffolding were in widespread use. Ports such as Lothal in Gujarat were used as export centers for trade with the rest of the world. The main goods were products created from smelted copper and bronze.

Kautilya's Arthashastra, written sometime in 300 BC, is a treatise of management in different spheres such as technology, economics, finance, military, and politics. It describes deep structures and processes that assist a king in managing a kingdom. Nagarjuna, another writer from ancient India, wrote the *Rasvatnakar* in 50 BC, and mentions distillation of zinc in Zawar, Rajasthan. Excavations conducted by the M.S. University of Vadodara in the region have revealed kilns used for zinc distillation. There is evidence that suggests that there was very little government interference with the world of business and trade. The numerous guilds that dotted the ancient Indian landscape—those run by painters, carpenters, smiths etc.—functioned under the leadership of a president. The only function of the government and the king appeared to be in the laying of roads to facilitate easy and efficient transportation.

Alexander's records describe, in great detail, a road that went from Penkelaotis (Pushkalavati) through Takshila to Pataliputra after crossing the river Beas.

Another road connected Pushkalavati to Indraprastha and then travelled downwards past the Vindhya ranges toward the Deccan Plateau, over the rivers Narmada and Tapti.

In Greek literature too, we see mentions of ancient India's manufacturing and trading prowess. Indian exports included a variety of spices, aromatics, quality textiles, ivory, iron, and gems. In return, Greece supplied cut gems, perfumes, wine, copper, and lead. The balance of trade was in India's favor, procuring from Greece a net payment of over fifty million sestertii in gold and silver coinage.

Medieval times in India were characterized by rulers who were scholarly, and gave great patronization to the arts and sciences. Raja Bhoja (1018–1060) of Dhar-Malwa designed and managed the construction of Bhojsagar, one of the largest artificial irrigation lakes of Medieval India. He also started a university called Bhojshala and in his magnum opus, *Somarangana Sutradhara,* provided a detailed blueprint for a network of roads connecting villages and towns in his kingdom.

The Iron Pillar of Delhi, at 23 feet and made of 99.72 percent wrought iron, which stands even today without any signs of rust or repair, is a great example of how developed metallurgical science was in our country in the middle ages. There are various mentions of steel production and zinc extraction in the books of various medieval writers. For example, Abul Fazal, the chief minister in Akbar's court, wrote in *Ain-e-Akbari* of how copper vessels could be coated with tin. Captain Presgrave of the Sagar Mint wrote in his report of the wrought iron bars and rods that he had commissioned:

"The iron is of the most excellent quality, possessing all the desirable properties of malleability, ductility at different temperatures, and tenacity for all of which I think it cannot be surpassed by the best Swedish iron."

Even in the textile industry, by 1700, India was the largest exporter to the world. The cotton goods industry became the largest employer of labor after agriculture. Visitors to the subcontinent were fascinated by the *perfection of the manufacturer* and the *simplicity of the tools*.

In spite of all these developments in ancient and medieval times, India somehow completely missed the Industrial Revolution that was gaining ground in Europe. Indian life in these times was relatively comfortable for the common man owing to the trade surpluses that led to high amounts of wealth. The education system—built around Gurukuls and Madarasas—became orthodox and resistant to change. Especially after the British colonization, education for the masses became so scant that the industries of India were pushed into a dark age.

In contrast, life in Europe during the medieval times was not easy. Harsh winters ravaged the land every year and trade deficits meant that the average man had to undergo hardships to survive. Such an environment proved conducive to revolution. Education got liberated from the clutches of the Christian church and a more innovative and scientific society developed from the sweat and tears of the people, ushering Europe into the golden age.

Independent India began life as an agrarian economy with almost zero industrial development. Only four or five big cities covered the large land mass, and a handful of industries made their presence felt only in these urban pockets. Export strategy was terribly exploitative, since it was set by the ruling British to exploit the raw materials and sell the finished goods to their colonies. Social indicators were poor. The government's first task was to improve social and material conditions of the people, and ignite the sleeping economy.

The current picture of Indian manufacturing is a story of two contrasting halves. In the first half, the successful half, lays the industries of IT, pharmaceuticals, automobiles, and Fast Moving Consumer Goods (FMCG) and in the dark half, we have sectors such as heavy engineering, chemicals, and small scale manufacturing. While the first half has benefited from liberalization and foreign inflows of cash, the second half has struggled under pressure from the global economy, much of which is decades ahead in terms of technology.

The biggest problem facing Indian manufacturing sector is two-fold: on one hand, we face competition for low-priced, mass consumption goods from the Chinese and Asian markets that fight us on price. On the other hand, we face competition for quality consumer goods from developed economies that fight us on superior technology and quality.

For instance if you look at the TVS group, you will see how it has grown from humble beginnings, and achieved remarkable scale, diversification, brand value and market prominence. Over decades, the group has gained the trust of millions in India and abroad. To my mind here's what I believe helped them make this journey:

1. A deep understanding of the customer and the market
2. Confidence and a belief in the organization's capability without a global partner
3. The willingness to take risks
4. Relentless focus on quality
5. Focus on building the TVS brand

On the other hand, HMT, once a brand that enjoyed near monopoly in its space, is a casualty of its own culture. What went wrong? Here's what I think:

1. Complacency due to its initial success as the first mover in a pre-liberalized economy
2. The company missed the digital watch revolution and just watched as other players made their moves
3. Bureaucracy and slow decision making
4. An inward looking approach when a keen eye on market trends and the competition was needed
5. A culture of entitlement; not uncommon in many organizations even today

(A more detailed background of these companies is included in Appendix 1)

CHAPTER FOUR

Management in India - Hospitality and the BPO Industry

'Athithi Devo Bhava'

Perhaps no industry in India is as old as the hospitality industry. Treating guests like God is present in our very ancient texts, and we've always considered hospitality to be one of our most important virtues. In most homes across the country, even during times when people had to struggle to assemble a meal for their own family members; guests and strangers got a warm bed to sleep in and they were well looked after. The value was *even if we starve, we will not turn away a guest from the door.*

In our history, the concept of shelter for travelers is not new. Way before travel became the multibillion dollar industry that it is today, humble wayfarers set forth on foot from their villages in search of adventure and wonder. These walkers needed to find shelter at least once a day, and they needed to find food at least three times a day.

Up cropped inns, viharas, dharamshalas, sarais, musafirkhanas—whatever name they were called by—they were places of eating, freshening up, and having shelter for wearied travelers.

On most of the well-travelled routes, these shacks and hovels arose right from the time of ancient Buddhist monks, through the Mughal period, to the present day. Somewhere along the line, travelers became wealthier, so the places in which they preferred to stay became more luxurious. The rich travelers refused to stay in the same dingy huts as the lower class people did, and they were willing to pay a higher price for the privilege of being treated like kings. So the hotels became diversified too, each catering to their own client demographic.

The modern history of Indian hotels began with the establishment of the Taj Mahal Hotel in Mumbai, in 1904, by Jamshedji Tata. Until then, much of the hospitality landscape was littered with western style hotels, which aimed to give the privileged class in India a taste of Western life. These hotels were targeted toward princes, kings and other high officers of the state.

What Jamshedji Tata did with the Taj Mahal hotel was to flip it around. He proffered to present the Indian way of life to travelers visiting the country from abroad. Right in those early years, he anticipated that having hotels that reflected the charm and character of India was important for the nation's image and development.

Today, the Taj Group of Hotels, held under the gambit of the Indian Hotel Company, owns up to of fifty-five properties across the country. In many ways, the story of India's rise as an economy could be mirrored by the tale of the rise of the Taj Group of Hotels.

Taj's success can be attributed to its customer focus, extremely high quality standards, inclusion of international best practices in conjunction with Indian values, employee focus, staff training, brand positioning, and strategic awareness for accurate market positioning.

On the other hand, the India Tourism Development Corporation (ITDC) can be seen in clear juxtaposition. It was set up in 1966 as a corporation under the Indian Companies Act of 1956, with the merger of Janpath Hotel India Ltd. and India Tourism Transport Undertaking Ltd. ITDC provides a complete range of tourism services, including accommodation, catering, entertainment, shopping, hotel consultancy, duty free shops, and an in-house travel agency. In 2002, the Government of India decided to disinvest in many public sector undertakings. ITDC was one of them.

Today the government has an equity participation of 51 percent in ITDC and the corporation has 49 percent equity participation. Despite the fact that it still caters to a section of tourists and travelers, the story of ITDC is one of missed opportunities, low quality standards, and a confused journey of government's high involvement and low participation. ITDC's failure can be attributed to the organization's bureaucracy, bloated work force, entitlement culture and unionization, lack of customer focus, and the failure to see that great buildings and property don't guarantee happy customers.

A Short History of the BPO Industry in India

In the early 1980s, British Airways, Britain's biggest airline, opened a small branch in Delhi as a back office for a few business process operations. Their intention was to leverage the low cost and high labor that Delhi offered in the hope of improving the efficiency and cost-effectiveness of some of their processes.

Unwittingly, they started an industry in India that would, in thirty years, change the face of the country and grow to be a significant contributor to the GDP. They started what is called the BPO (Business Process Outsourcing) industry, establishing India as the favorite outsourcing hub for the entire world.

In the second half of the 1980s, American Express set up back office operations in Gurgaon. In the 1990s, General Electric came to the city and set up a branch. Called GECIS (General Electric Capital International Services), they were the first to try voice operations out of India, and they were so pleased with the results that over the next ten years, they ramped up their India presence and registered GECIS as a separate company: Genpact.

The IT boom then brought in the second wave of development in the BPO industry. Multinational IT companies entered India and bought out established, homegrown BPOs. (Example, the acquisition of Daksh by IBM.) Some of them like Accenture, HP, and Dell, came and set up service arms of their respective companies in India, extending the reach of BPO from customer service and telemarketing toward more extensive services like consulting, product development, and testing.

Today, nearly 75 percent of European multinational companies and the U.S., use outsourcing or shared services, and at least 71 percent of these companies are expected to continue using outsourcing till 2020.

Though a certain segment of the BPO industry has transitioned into higher order services like consulting, much of it is still engaged in fulfilling the basic needs like telemarketing and call centers. These organizations typically offered jobs to young graduates and trained them to speak in English using Western accents and names. When a washing machine acted up somewhere in North Dakota, and when the customer called their toll free customer care number, the call was transferred to an office in Bangalore, where a girl in her early twenties would answer and introduce herself as Rachel. (Her real name would be Rashmi or something.)

These and more features of the typical BPO organization gave rise to its own unique work culture. For perhaps the first time, companies of a sector were employing almost exclusively young people and were overpaying them for their qualification and experience. For perhaps the first time, management structures needed to break away from their hierarchical roots and become flatter, more cooperative, and more inclusive.

Let's take a quick look at Genpact and what made it so successful. Genpact began in 1997 as a business processing unit (called GE capital International services (GECIS) within General Electric. It started with the mandate to provide business process services to GE capital's businesses globally. Over the years, even through the ups and downs, the company has stayed the course, shown massive growth, and delivered a wide suite of services. This has been possible because it realized the value of its workforce, ensured robust people engagement systems, and reinvented itself in terms of people, processes, and market focus.

How did Genpact manage to thrive in the midst of a dynamic market? Of course, they were the pioneers in the BPO space. They had some of the most admired systems and processes, and they pursued a strategy that helped them achieve scale rapidly. More fundamentally though, it is their focus on people that enabled them to create an employee friendly culture, attract the best talent, train and motivate people, enable gender diversity, and offer rewards and recognition for top performers in the process of building a culture of excellence.

CHAPTER FIVE

Management in India - The Indian IT Industry

Sometime in the early part of this millennium, in the year 2000 or 2001, the Government of India coined a phrase to help it get re-elected to power. The phrase was 'India Shining'. In the decade 1993–2002, India grew at an average rate of 6 percent per annum, which led the rest of the world sit up and take notice. They called us an emerging nation, a high growth region.

Today, we've managed to sustain that growth in spite of a few hiccups here and there. We're now part of the BRICS block (Brazil, Russia, India, China and South Africa), which is growing in geopolitical power thanks to the rapidly evolving economic fundamentals of its members.

Going by most financial and political commentators, India is the country to watch out for in the next twenty years. Not only do we have a robust growth history, but we also have what is called the demographic dividend. The median age of India's population is 28, significantly lower than China's 37.6 and Japan's 44.4.

And perhaps, most crucially, we also have our IT industry.

In 1998, the IT industry made up 1.2 percent of India's GDP. In 2012, its share was 7.5 percent. The sector garnered U.S. $132billion in revenues in 2015 and is growing at an annual rate of 9 percent, outstripping any other industry in the country.

The story of the IT boom in India began in 1991, when the Government of India introduced liberalization reforms in order to aid the flagging state of the country's economy and industry. The goal was to make the economy more market oriented and to increase the involvement of foreign markets. Import tariffs were reduced, markets were deregulated, taxes were revisited, and foreign investments were encouraged.

The first major IT reform by the Indian Government came as part of the liberalization process, with the setting up of a corporation called Software Technology Parks of India (STPI). This corporation provided satellite links to major software companies in India, which enabled them to deliver work overseas without fearing loss of information or security. This also improved the trust of countries, such as the United States of America, in India's ability to deliver and its suitability as an outsource destination.

The business model in the IT industry is similar to that of BPOs. All the high-end work such as software architecture, design, and requirements gathering are done at the client's location, whereas all the low-end work such as development and testing are outsourced to India. This is similar to a BPO situation, where corporations treat their Indian branches as back offices.

However, this reality is changing with more Indian professionals going overseas to work on temporary assignments and bringing back their experience to India. The level of trust in the quality of work that India can produce is climbing steadily, and many high-end jobs are being outsourced to Indian branches of multinational software giants.

IBM has recently taken a step to address this very issue. Until 2013, the official policy within the company had been that the Indian team should consider the on-shore team as a client. However, starting from 2013, they were to be considered partners, as equals. This step was taken to weed out the feeling of inferiority that was taking root in the culture of their Indian offices, especially in their transactions with IBM colleagues situated elsewhere in the world.

More companies will follow suit in IBM's path, and it will not be surprising if at some point in the future, India will provide end-to-end software solutions to the rest of the world, from design to delivery.

The IT industry is probably the most suited example for the phenomenon of knowledge and mental skills replacing physical labor and experience. It is not uncommon to find a person fresh out of college demonstrating better technical abilities than his manager, or his team lead who is more experienced.

Also, since technology is changing so fast, the employees who let their capabilities rust without updating them are bound to find themselves being overtaken by younger, sharper minds. The importance of keeping oneself up to date with technology is more important in the IT field than it is elsewhere.

IT is also the field of specialization. There are database experts, front-end designers, UI developers, manual testers, automated testers, business analysts, requirements gatherers, application architects, enterprise architects and so on. It's not unusual to see all of these people working together in one team on any given IT project. And on top of this diverse set of workers sits the project manager, who must not only know enough about each role to be able to converse with them, but he must also understand the importance of being *the dumb person in a room full of smart people*, because he often has to take advice from his resources about technical matters that he doesn't have enough knowledge about.

On the other hand, he drives the delivery of a project, and he takes the final decisions. He is accountable. Therefore, a manager of an IT project must forever tread this fine line consulting with the experts in his team, deferring to their better judgment, but also ensuring that his own personality and decision-making does not get affected.

The third thing he must do with aplomb—or at least with adequacy—is to allow the different specialists in his team to communicate with one another. It is quite common for people who have deeply studied one aspect of their craft to develop tunnel vision and to miss the bigger picture. So developers may not see eye to eye with testers. Database administrators may play hardball with architects. Often teams talk *at* each other, not *to* each other. So the manager must be a pacifier at these times, a generalist leader in a team full of specialists.

Perhaps more than any IT company in India, Infosys has enjoyed the reputation of being one of the most respected brands not just within the industry but also across industries. Set up in 1981 with a capital of INR 10,000 the company has grown into a veritable giant spanning solutions, services, and products and catering to some of the most reputed clients across industries in every corner of the world. What accounts for this company's almost miraculous success? First, they were the pioneers in the IT off-shoring model and eventually they became the face of the Indian IT industry. They ensured the DNA in the core team of leaders didn't change too much over the years. They invested in the right people, built world class infrastructure, empowered people with training, attractive compensation and benefits, and constantly revisited their strategic assumptions to remain agile, forward-looking and market ready.

CHAPTER SIX

Management in India - Comparative Analysis

In this chapter, we will collate the information that we've gleaned from the three previous chapters to perform a comparative analysis of the four industries. I hope that this will give us a reasonably complete picture of management in India, both from a historical context, and how it appears and works in the present day.

UNMANAGE

I have produced my analysis in the table below.

Comparison of Key parameters

	Hiearchy	Accountability	Resistance to change	Control	Average Manager age
Mftg-PSU	High	Low	High	High	45+
Mftg-Pvt	High	High	Medium	High	40+
BPO	High	High	Low	High	25+
IT	Low	High	Low	Low	30+
Hospitality-Pvt	High	High	Medium	High	40+
Hospitality-PSU	High	Low	High	High	45+

This image of a turtle on a post eloquently captures the way people get promoted to management for the wrong reasons.

Post Turtle

- "You know he didn't get up there by himself, he doesn't belong up there, he doesn't know what to do while he's up there,
- he's elevated beyond his ability to function,
- and you just wonder what kind of dumb ass put him up there to begin with."

Copyright Naresh Purushotham, Author,
Not for circulation

CHAPTER SEVEN

The Cultural Implications of Being a Manager in India

Factors Influencing the Indian Manager

India is a patriarchal, class based, hierarchical society. I won't go into a discussion of whether or not that is good. In our family units, there is a clear head (the father), and in our social structure, there is a clear framework on which group of people stand where on the ladder. Brahmins are supposed to be superior to everyone else, then the Kshatriyas, then the Vysyas, and then the Shudras.

We differentiate ourselves in many ways—by language, by caste, by religion, by economic status, and by gender. Moreover, whenever there are divisions made, the first question that crops up is, *"Who, whose is better?"*

In such a society, is it any surprise that there is a mad rush, an absolute craze at the workplace, to become a manager? Because being a manager, means that you're the leader, that you're the one making the rules, that you're *superior* to your underlings. For people raised on values that worship social hierarchy, such thinking is inevitable.

The role of a manager therefore comes with connotations of worship and respect. This is why the parents of the young man I was referring to earlier have such pride in their voices when they announced that their son had become a manager. He's not just a team member any more, they think, he's the leader. He's the one who orders people around. He's the one who sits back in his plush cabin with his feet up on the table while his subordinates scurry around to obey his commands.

Then there is the question of money. On average, managers earn more than the people they manage. This is not always true in the West, where technical career paths are available, where it is not uncommon to find a twenty-four year old managing a fifty-year-old veteran in the field. However, in India, the manager is almost always older and more experienced than his team members. It just aligns well with our ideas of seniority and respect.

The diagram below shows how ridiculous management structures warp any sense of fairness we hope to have.

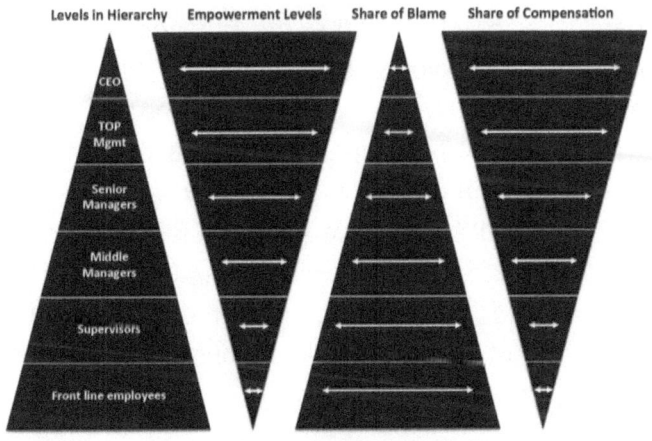

Copyright Naresh Purushotham, Author,
Not for circulation

We don't find it easy to respect someone younger than us in real life. Therefore, we stay away from the concept in our working lives too. We have a set career path for almost everyone passing through the industry—work in a technical field for five years, perhaps six, and then take up a management role. Make your way up the ladder steadily, accumulating age, experience, and—in theory at least—wisdom.

This rigid pecking order gives rise to a deep fear of one's manager. It is possible for employees today to respect their managers, but fear comes first. Indeed, in our culture, it is often proclaimed that respect is impossible without fear. Therefore, the employee fears every meeting he has with his manager. Every time he is called into a room, he's thinking, "Oh, no, what have I done now?"

There is also a feeling that the manager holds the reins of the employee's career in his hands. The employee feels powerless, as though he's a puppet being played by a master. If we take a walk through the cafeterias in our companies today, where people gather and talk socially, we will find a healthy number of people shrugging helplessly—with respect to salary hikes and promotions, most often—and saying, "All of this is just a lie. If your manager wants to help you, he will find a way."

This attitude gives rise on the other end of the spectrum to people who use sycophancy to further their careers. How often have we not heard stories of this or that employee who has done his or her manager certain favors in return for a raise? We may dismiss them as cock-and-bull stories. We may laugh when exaggerated forms of sycophancy are depicted in movies and literature. Nevertheless, there is no smoke without fire.

The deeper we allow this culture of sycophancy to develop, the more we lose the trust of our team members. A team that believes that sucking up to the boss is more important than turning in good work; will always underperform, because they're focused on the wrong thing. Moreover, if your team underperforms, so will you.

But how do we overcome this? How do we change our management structures so that they bring the ability of the employee into focus? How do we turn ourselves into managers that are not feared by our wards but respected, trusted and loved? Is it possible to build a management approach in India that aims to make the manager a friend of his team members without compromising on the quality of work produced?

My argument is yes, and I will propose one such approach in the next chapter.

Before that, I would like you to do this reflective exercise and ask yourself these questions and score them based on how you normally think and act.

Reflection Exercise – Choose One That Best Describes Your Current Managerial Style

1a. I consider myself part of the team.
1b. I consider myself as the manager of the team.
1c. I consider myself the power center.

2a. When people call me Sir or Madam, I consider it a mark of respect.
2b. I encourage people to call me by my first name.
2c. I prefer a Mr. or Ms. prefixed to my name.

3a. Without a clearly defined boss-subordinate structure, there will be a lot of confusion.
3b. Relationships are determined by the nature of work and projects.
3c. Look at how well the military functions. It is because of hierarchy.

4a. An organization chart clearly establishes reporting relationships.
4b. An organization chart shows who's who in organizations.
4c. People are banded and disbanded according to customer requirements.

5a. I need to maintain a distance from my subordinates.
5b. I believe that I am a member of my team.
5c. I hang out with my folks.

6a. People work for money.
6b. People work to get promoted.
6c. People work because they love to.

7a. The more experienced you are, the more valuable you are.
7b. It is what you contribute that matters.
7c. It is all about the quality of ideas you bring to the table.

8a. Office politics is a fact of life.
8b. It is possible to build an environment of trust, respect, and transparency.
8c. A few trusted people give me the information I need to know.

9a. The younger generation lacks discipline and commitment.
9b. The younger generation is a highly talented lot.
9c. The younger generation teaches me lots of stuff I don't know.

10a. To get things done, I must closely follow up and control.
10b. To get things done I just need to define the outcomes and get out of the way.

10c. To get things done ask a lot of questions, listen, be open and be there.

How to calculate your score:

1 a) = 3 2a) = 0 3a) = 1 4a) = 1 5a) = 0 6a) = 1
1 b) = 1 2b) = 3 3b) = 3 4b) = 1 5b) = 2 6b) = 2
1 c) = 0 2c) = 1 3c) = 0 4c) = 3 5c) = 3 6c) = 3
7a) = 0 8a) = 0 9a) = 0 10a) = 1
7b) = 2 8b) = 3 9b) = 2 10b) = 2
7c) = 3 8c) = 0 9c) = 3 10c) = 3

Score:

10 – Yesterday's Manager
10–15 – Between Yesterday and Today
15–20 – Today's manager
20–25 – Between today and tomorrow
25–30 – You are there!

CHAPTER EIGHT

Management for Today's World

In this chapter, I will introduce a new approach to management called the management effectiveness model, based around three core values and three dimensions. The three core values are:

1. Integrity
2. Trust
3. Credibility

The three dimensions, in order of importance, are:

1. Relationships
2. Tasks
3. Results

A pictorial representation is below. The top circle rests on a central anvil of integrity, trust, and credibility, which are the non-negotiable core values any manager must seek to develop. In dimensionality, relationships take more importance over tasks, which take more importance over results. This is in sharp contrast to present-day management practice, where managers generally become so result-oriented that they ignore more important attributes such as relationships.

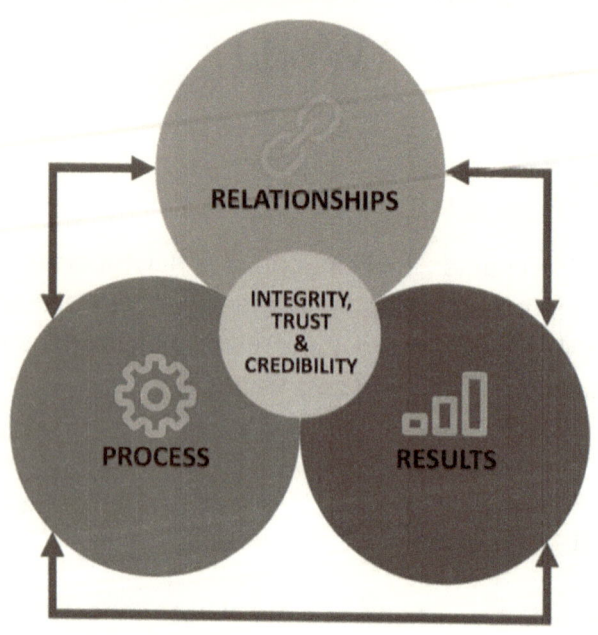

The double-headed arrows in the figure, which travels between the three dimensions, show their interdependence on each other. Therefore, the way in which we manage our relationships will have a bearing on the tasks and the results, and the way in which we manage our tasks and results will have a direct bearing on the relationships we foster with our team members.

Through the course of this chapter, let's take a look at each of the three dimensions in isolation. In the next three chapters, we will devote all of our energies to the core values, integrity, trust, and credibility. Then, in the following three chapters, we will look at how combinations of these dimensions give rise to other key attributes that every manager must develop within herself and within her team.

More specifically:
- The combination of relationships and results will be the theme of the chapter on transparency.
- The combination of relationships and process will be the theme of the chapter on motivation.
- The combination of process and results will be the theme of the chapter on delegation.

Every manager, by her nature, will gravitate toward one of the three dimensions proposed in this model. You may naturally be inclined to be more relationship-focused in your management style, or you may be focused on tasks, believing that your team members need to be micromanaged. Alternatively, you may be the *freethinking* manager, communicating purely results and letting your team figure out the details.

There is no right or wrong answer here, so the purpose of this chapter is not to glorify one style over the other. Each has its benefits and its disadvantages. I'm going to propose that you need to figure out a healthy balance of the three that is right for your personality. I will not prescribe a certain combination for you because I don't know you well enough.

Let us then look at each of the dimensions in turn and evaluate them objectively, so that we can first lay out all the pros and cons on the table. We can then proceed to make our choice.

The relationships-focused manager
(The Popular Manager)

The manager who is relationship-focused will yearn to know what it is that makes her employees tick not just professionally but also personally. She will typically be a friendly person by nature. Empathy comes to her easily. She cares for her team's emotional health, knows all of them by first name, keeps a working knowledge of what is happening in their daily lives, and acts as a personal mentor in addition to a work manager.

Being relationship-focused in your management style needs a lot of investment in time. You will need to break through the professional barrier and be a personal friend to each of your employees. This means that you will need to spend a lot of one-on-one time, not just in meetings but also in social settings such as lunch and tea breaks at work. The better you allow your team members to get to know you, the more they will feel comfortable around you.

Pros:

- This management style generally makes for happy teams. It contributes to the personal growth of both manager and employee.
- Since the manager knows each of her employees intimately, she is better able to design roles for them that suit their aspirations and needs.

- The manager finds it easier to motivate her employees and maximize the potential of each.

Cons:

- The manager can become over sympathetic and start lowering the employee's standards.
- It could lead to a country club team culture, where the employees start to take advantage of the manager's apparent laid back nature.
- The performance of the team—in terms of results—may suffer.

One of the finest Managerial Leaders I have met in the course of my work is Mr. Suresh Kumar, CEO, ITC - Fortune Hotels.

He role models a number of qualities but the one thing that stands out for me is his ability to build and nurture human relationships. In addition, he does that at all levels from the doorman to his GMs!

For starters, he has a penchant for names and recalls names even if he bumps into people years later.

He knows people's personal contexts—spouse, children, their education, many times even their parents. I have often heard him say things like "How is your Dad doing after the heart surgery?"

When he greets his people, he always gives them a hug and a very animated greeting. I recall once a housekeeper he was meeting after many years and she hugged him for what seemed like forever and broke into tears!

He took a genuine interest in every person he interacted with in his team.

While he loves them, he never ever allows people to become lax at what they have to deliver. In fact, if anything, his folks would go out of the way to deliver excellence!

The opposite of this example is what I have seen on many occasions. The relationship focus descending into a cozy country club atmosphere where the work suffers. I recall a manager who would go to great lengths to keep his people happy. He would know their personal problems and challenges and often got involved in discussing and also resolving them. And clearly, he had team members who would take advantage of him. He had a team member who was a chronic case. This person would come late, miss deliverables, do a shoddy job. Whenever on rare occasions when he mustered enough courage to pull up this person, the team member would retort by saying "How can you ask me even after knowing my condition?" and this manager would instantly back off. The result was that he ended up having to do all the work!

One of the reasons a relationship-focused manager is also a popular manager is because it is the right kind of management style to possess as long as she is focused on tasks along with results. A relationship-focused manager is people-oriented. If you get the people equation right, tasks and results will automatically follow.

JRD Tata who was the chairman of Tata Group was a renowned relationship-focused manager. There are several stories of JRD Tata's association with his employees that many fondly recall. One of them is Sudha Murthy, Narayana Murthy's wife. Between 1974 and 1982, she worked at TELCO (Tata Engineering and Locomotive Company) in Mumbai. One day, after work, she was waiting for Narayana Murthy to pick her up. It was late and surprisingly, she saw JRD Tata standing next to her. He asked,

"Young lady, what are you doing here?" She replied that office time was over and she was waiting for her husband to pick her up. He decided to wait with her as it was getting dark and there was no one around. Sudha Murthy was taken aback to see a respectable industrialist waiting for the sake of an ordinary employee. Soon Narayana Murthy made an appearance and JRD Tata said to Sudha Murthy, "Young lady, tell your husband never to make his wife wait again."

Another example is Russi Mody, former chairman of Tata Steel. He would say, "What is man management? That one must behave naturally with any human being." He would always listen to his employees and note their concerns, often raising genuine ones with their managers. Highly perceptive, he had a finger on the pulse of his people. If he missed wishing someone on his or her birthday, he would run up and apologize for forgetting. Under his leadership, Tata Steel grew leaps and bounds. Ratan Tata mentioned that Russi Mody was an institution at Tata Steel.

It is great to be relationship-focused but managers need to pull in the reins if they find themselves losing focus on tasks and results. The effective relationship manager is someone who walks the tight rope between building strong relationships along with building a culture of accountability.

The process-focused manager
(The Taskmaster)

The kind of person who gravitates naturally toward being task-focused is typically an over achiever who has set ideas in her head about *how things need to be done*. So not only is she focused on the result, but she also spends a lot of time in thinking about exactly how to achieve this result. She believes in breaking the bigger problem down into manageable tasks, and then following up each task to its completion.

Being task-focused requires you as the manager to understand with a reasonable level of intimacy every step of the solution. You will sit next to developers and work through some lines of code. You will meet with your testers and review their work products. You will meet with designers, architects, business analysts, and with every group in your team and find out how they're doing things. When you think they're on the wrong path, you advise, you caution, you guide.

This will put enormous pressures on your time, but you will be rewarded by an intimate knowledge of the whole system and a unique roadmap ahead where you can plan for hurdles more proactively.

Pros:

- The task-focused manager is generally a knowledgeable manager. She's always on top of things, and at any point in time, she knows what each of her team is doing and what progress has been made.
- Being task-focused gives the manager a unique big picture view of everything going on in her project. She is less likely to be taken by surprise by unforeseen occurrences. She gets an early sighting of any dependencies and is able to plan for them better.
- A task-based approach helps in treating the final result as a consequence, thereby reducing the pressure on both the manager and the team.

Cons:

- The team views the manager as interfering, and as a micromanager.
- Since the manager is taking care of the big picture, teams are liable to become specialized and work with tunnel vision. Over time, they lose the ability to keep the whole project in mind and become focused only on their particular task.
- It can lead to situations where your team has lost touch with each other. For example, testers can begin testing code that is not even ready. Developers can begin coding on a piece of work where design is not yet complete.

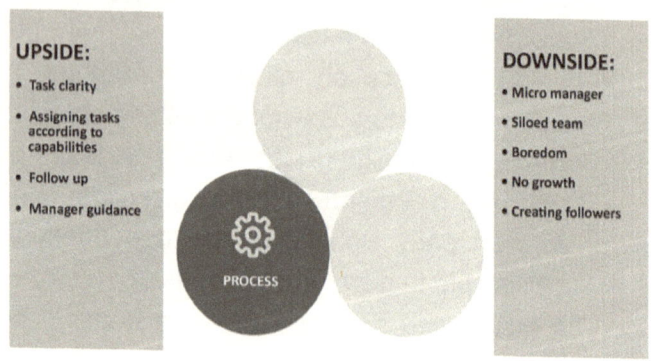

To demonstrate how task-focused management works, imagine two men digging holes on the side of a road. One is digging holes with his crowbar steadily removing mud and throwing it to one side, while the other picks up the same mud and covers the holes dug by the first man. This activity continues for a while and a bystander who has been watching them is thoroughly puzzled. He knows it does not make sense. He approaches the two men and asks them, "What are you guys up to?" The two men explain that they have a third person on their team who is supposed to plant saplings in each of the holes but he is on leave. However, they cannot stop working because the man who digs holes is paid for the number of holes that he digs and the man who fills them up is paid for the number of holes that he covers. Thus, both men are performing the required tasks but the purpose is lost. They might be working toward a greater goal of planting trees and protecting the environment but they fail to see the big picture because their manager is focused on the tasks that need to be performed. She has not explained to the workers the importance of their job or its impact in future. Ideally, she should have told them that their contribution today would be recognized fifty years later when these saplings grow into trees.

Managers are often in a hurry and they want individual tasks to be completed. They step into a room and tell people what they need to do without trying to connect with them or have them understand the big picture. Typically, task-focused managers can be found more often in support functions within organizations such as finance, accounts, or HR.

They focus on process and tasks above everything else.

In 2017, a human resource executive from Tech Mahindra fired one of its IT professionals asking him to put his papers down by the end of the day, failing which he would receive a termination notice from the company. A leaked audio clip of the HR person speaking to the distressed employee went viral causing uproar in the media. While you can hear the HR executive say that the company is focusing on cost optimization due to which several employees would be asked to leave, her indifference and lack of empathy is evident. All that the employee was asking for was an extra day! However, for the HR Executive, she had to meet her daily target of exits!

Finally, the fiasco forced the Chairman Anand Mahindra to issue a public apology.

The results-focused manager
(The Transactional Manager)

Many of the managers in the current Indian corporate scenario are result-focused. Indeed, this is sensible because in the cutthroat world of revenues and profits, it is results that matter. Nobody ever pays anyone for the effort they put in. Money changes hands when results are achieved. More money is paid when better results are achieved.

In the collectivist culture that is India, for the majority of people, results are taken care of by someone else. Your typical employee is unlikely to care about the project's overall goals. She will be more interested in finding out from you what she needs to do. In such an environment, where no one keeps an eye on the results, it makes sense for the manager to take the reins and hold them tight.

Therefore, a results-focused manager will communicate results to her employees over tasks. She will spend less of her time understanding the solution her team is providing and spend more time tracking the overall progress of the project. She will take undue care to ask her team to raise dependencies early so that she could remove them. She will place most of the risk avoidance in her team's hands, and will dedicate herself to making the path as smooth as she can for her team.

Pros:

- The team feels empowered because the manager takes advice from them. It forces the team to think of the overall project, and communication between teams is often good under a results-focused manager.
- Teams work smart, not hard.
- Wasteful, non-value adding work is eliminated because communication channels within the team are robust and functional.

Cons:

- It's possible to adopt a shortsighted nature where results become *everything*. Companies can fall into the rut of focusing exclusively on quarterly results.
- You become transactional in your dealing with your employees, fraying the relationship you have with them.
- Your team may burn out because you're constantly pushing them to achieve the result no matter what.
- You may be tempted to use hire and fire policies, which will affect the long-term health and morale of your team.

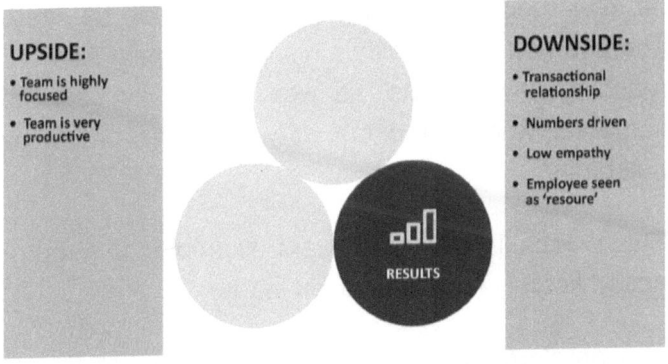

Results-focused managers are interested in the end game. How you are feeling, your situation, whether you are happy or unhappy—the transactional manager is not concerned. This behavior could extend to the point of slave driving. Typically, these managers are found in the IT industry working as project managers. Their objective is to achieve results! Bob Johnson, a famous speaker, aptly summarizes a results-focused manager's approach. This manager tells his people, "Don't tell me about the labor pain; show me the baby!"

You might recognize Jack Welch as the former chairman of General Electric who was famously nicknamed 'Neutron Jack'. Now, he is a typical example of a results-focused manager. His *mantra* was simple, "It is either my way or the highway." He was known to pull people up, give orders, and expect it to be done immediately. He acknowledged that he lost his temper several times early in his career. According to him, well-performing employees must be rewarded, and inefficient ones must be fired. There is no midway. While his management saw GE reaching new heights, he was universally seen as someone who lacked empathy and was driven by outcomes.

Steve Jobs is a more recent example of a hard-nosed fiercely results-focused leader.

The problem with results-focused managers is that they play tennis with their eyes fixed on the scoreboard instead of the ball. However, you don't win matches by focusing on the scoreboard; you have to focus on the ball and the scoreboard will take care of itself.

Self-assessment

As we discussed at the beginning of the chapter, this is not an exercise in judgment. We're not criticizing one type of manager and praising the others. Clearly, all three dimensions—relationships, tasks, and results—ought to be focused on in order for us to be effective managers. But the truth is that depending on your personality and character, you will naturally sway toward one over the other two. Working consciously to develop the 'hidden' facets of your management style will make you a better, well-rounded manager.

In this section, therefore, I've included a short questionnaire, which will give you a 360-degree view of your management style. I recommend that you take it, and if possible, get your colleagues to respond to the survey as well.

Self-assessment questionnaire:

	Rate Yourself on a scale of 1–5 on how frequently you demonstrate the indicated behavior	Score
	1 - Never, 2 - Rarely, 3 - Usually, 4 - Often, 5 - Always	
	Open and Effective Communication	
1	Communicates with clarity, is precise, and makes an impact.	
2	Uses sensitivity and discretion with decisions and recommendations that are perceived as negative.	
3	Explains abstract concepts with examples, relevant information, and data.	
	Emotional intelligence	
4	Is aware of his / her emotional states at all times.	
5	Manages own emotions well and is even tempered in all circumstances.	
6	Easily recognizes emotional fluctuations in others and prepares to address them.	
	Collaboration	
7	Takes ownership for work organization and collaborating efforts of the team.	
8	Defines the team goals and objectives clearly.	
9	Elicits ideas from the team and involves them in discussions and listens to them.	
10	Adjusts wherever needed and brings in new ideas to meet team goals.	
11	Encourages team to perform at their peak by involving them and recognizes team efforts.	

	Reward 'n' Recognition	
12	Initiates periodic performance related discussions with team members and establishes objectives, which are growth oriented for both the individual and the organization.	
13	Sets aside quality time for performance discussions, begins on a positive note and listens intently to the team member's perspectives.	
14	Is able to give realistic feedback as and when required and ensures performance gaps are addressed in a timely manner.	
15	Identifies relevant reward mechanisms and acknowledges contributions appropriately.	
16	Understands what specifically motivates each team member and takes the effort to tailor recognition initiatives accordingly.	
	Accountability	
17	Is goal oriented and consistently delivers results.	
18	Takes ownership and responsibility for own work.	
19	Team members feel they have contributed to the results achieved.	
	Defines & Communicates Vision	
20	Has a clear vision for the team or function and sees the bigger picture.	
21	Clearly articulates the vision to the team.	
22	Frequently highlights the connect between day-to-day tasks and the larger vision.	
23	Encourages team members to contribute to and participate in discussions around strategic goals.	
24	Clearly separately critical and non-critical activity based on relevance to vision.	
	Delegation & Empowerment	
25	Explains the benefits of the task when delegating a task to team members.	

26	Establishes key performance indicators when delegating a task.	
27	Ensures proper training to the delegates wherever and whenever needed.	
28	Identifies the right person for the task while delegating by considering his/her skills, knowledge, and attitude to perform well.	
29	Allows different points of view to be aired. Creates a "non-punishing" environment for idea exchange and gives specific feedback that covers positive points and areas of concern.	
	Managing Personal Time & Energy	
30	Prioritizes tasks and accomplishes that which needs to be done on schedule so that personal time can be well managed.	
31	Uses personal time in a planned manner with clear vision and objectives.	
32	Prioritizes personal tasks to focus on value add activities like family time, learning, rejuvenation, etc.	
33	Clearly marks boundaries between professional and personal commitments without compromising either.	
	Change Management	
34	Sets realistic targets and priorities for change.	
35	Anticipates specific reasons underlying resistance to change and implements approaches that address resistance.	
36	Manages time by prioritizing and organizing the changes.	
37	Involves employees in decisions.	
38	Sets clear deadlines.	
39	Tolerates honest mistakes as learning experiences.	
	Responsive Problem Solving	
40	Asks the right questions to find the root cause of	

	the problem.	
41	Examines problems from all angles before devising solutions.	
42	Solicits and examines alternative ideas before deciding on the best solution.	
43	Ensures that the solution resolves the problem entirely i.e. the problem does not recur.	
44	Chooses the most effective solution instead of the expedient one.	
	Total Score (out of a max of 220)*	

Legend: The higher the score, the more well-rounded you are as a Manager.

Final Words

An interesting point to note is that managers tend to become like their managers. Therefore, if you are a task-focused manager, you are likely to have had a task-focused manager. The same applies to results-focused managers and relationship-focused managers. Individuals learn management from their own managers leading to an imitative management style.

We've introduced a management effectiveness model designed to make us all better managers and better people. We've looked at each of the dimensions that make up the right approach—relationships, tasks, and results—and evaluated their pros and cons. Then we've taken the management assessment, so that we know where we stand, and where our natural inclinations lie.

In the next chapter, we will focus exclusively on the anvil of our approach, on the core values that will make up the foundation of your management strategy. They are integrity, trust, and credibility.

CHAPTER NINE

Integrity

In this chapter, we will look at the rather tricky concept of integrity. We all know the theoretical details of how to do the right thing, but we always fail in the practicalities. Therefore, in this chapter, I will try my best not to harp on about the mere commandments, but also introduce a few tricks and techniques that we can all use to put those theories into practice.

Integrity is not just one aspect of your behavior. It encompasses various behavioral traits like consistency, honesty, humility, and self-control. In fact, if integrity could be described in one word, it would be self-control. Because it's the temptation that lures us into being bad whether it is high bonuses, a better relationship with your manager at the cost of your colleagues, a harmless fling that your partner will not know about, or anything else.

If you can say no to temptation, you're already on your way to being a person of integrity. But let's not get ahead of ourselves. Let's first look at the many components that combine to form this elusive word called integrity.

The word integrity is related to the roots of words like 'integrate' and 'entire'. In Spanish, it is rendered *integro*, meaning whole. Integrity thus implies the state of being complete, undivided, intact, and unbroken. Such a state contrasts with one that is scattered, fragmented, and incomplete. If one were to go by the dictionary, therefore, integrity could be defined as the trait that allows you to be *consistent* in character, no matter what the situation.

The other word that comes to mind is *predictable*. But of course, one could be consistent and predictable for all the wrong reasons. Adolf Hitler must have been pretty predictable during his Third Reich days, and yet some people even argue that he is a man of integrity. So we must add to the qualities of consistency and predictability, some other standards of behavior that our society judges as right. The ego is the chief blocker in all these behaviors. Here are a few:

Courage to admit mistakes
A good manager never hesitates to come forward and say, "I goofed up. Sorry folks." This actually

makes the manager more endearing and more human.

The insecure, arrogant manager, on the contrary, tries to cover his tracks and starts to externalize his failure. Blame games, cover ups, etc. begin and people in his team take the blame.

I have made monumental mistakes in my life and it took me a while to admit that I was the central piece and until I faced it squarely, I couldn't come out of the difficult circumstances.

Willingness to apologize
Why is it so difficult for people to say sorry? I shouldn't be asking this, because my wife often reminds me how difficult it is for me to apologize after an argument! Added to this, is the courage to apologize in public.

The arrogant manager sees no reason to apologize. He thinks his seniority gives him that pass! The situation worsens when the top bosses ignore it and condone the manager's behavior.

I painfully recall an incident when I pulled up my then eight-year-old daughter in front of her friends for not sharing her gifts. Later that night I found her sobbing after her birthday party. I didn't realize that I had hurt her by scolding her in front of her friends. That night, I learnt the power of saying sorry!

Say what you do, do what you say (SWYDDWYS)
Perhaps the most difficult and easier said than done!

Great managers stand by their commitments—both professional and personal. If they promise something—big or small—they follow through.

Other managers are selective about SWYDDWYS. They keep their commitments to their higher-ups but ignore what they need to do for their team members or family members.

This is one area I can truly take pride in! I make it a point to follow through be it a fresher looking for a placement or a client asking for some information.

Willingness to bury the hatchet
Zig Ziglar says that forgiveness is important and it benefits the forgiver more than the person who has caused us pain.

I believe that we should forgive but not condone. It is important to move on, but only after a good discussion about the incident.

Someone said there are three truths to any situation. One is ours, the other person's truth, and finally the real truth!

I have seen great managers who deal with unfortunate situations where team members/peers/bosses have let them down very gracefully. They assertively bring it up, discuss it threadbare, and move on with no baggage.

Mediocre managers or toxic managers on the other hand, carry their grudges right into every discussion/meeting/water cooler conversations and into appraisals! And make sure that you pay the price for having wronged them.

Humility and modesty

Jim Collins in his timeless masterpiece *Good to Great* says that truly great success leaders typically attribute their success to luck and being in the right place at the right time. Even when there is enough evidence to prove that they played a significant role in steering their organizations.

Managers, who have achieved very little, indulge in chest thumping and try to garner all the credit.

Again, people gravitate toward managers who graciously acknowledge others and shy away from being in the spotlight.

Beware of the manager who says, "I am so humble!"

Gratitude and appreciation

Managers who have an attitude of gratitude in their lives learn to see the good things in life and are not cribbers. So many of us take our progress for granted and never pause to look at the ladder we have climbed. We don't acknowledge people who facilitated our climb. I keep hearing people say that they are self-made individuals. None of us are! Being grateful for what we are in our lives helps us to be content and in turn inspire others to stop chasing meaningless goals.

Of course, there's a balance to it. Still if I have to err, I would err on the side of over doing it.

Petty managers are stingy with praise and generous with criticism. I like the phrase *catch your people doing something right* as against *catch people doing something wrong*. My belief is that if you bring genuine appreciation into your management style, your people will do a lot more to ensure that nothing goes wrong.

Generosity and appreciation go together. Be grateful and appreciate at least one person each day in your team.

By the way, bosses and peers also crave for appreciation so don't ignore appreciation upwards and sideways!

The importance of role models
A great question to ask youngsters is, "*Name your role models.*"

Who do they aspire to become?

Sports people like Sachin Tendulkar, M S Dhoni. Musicians like Jesudas, M S Subbulakshmi, Corporate leaders like JRD Tata, Narayanamoorthy, Politicians (I will not name them for fear of controversy) have inspired countless people to achieve great things in their lives.

Having a role model is like holding a compass in your hands. Beware of the manager who says his boss is his role model. This maybe sycophancy at its best!

Decisiveness under pressure
Jack Welch known for his amazing speed in decision-making once famously said that indecision costs the organization more than wrong decisions.

This is great advice. I recently read a Jeff Bezos approach to decisions where he recommends that we differentiate between *reversible* and *irreversible* decisions. Irreversible decision-making must be done slowly but the other category, reversible, must be fast and quick.

Again, a good manager does not buckle under pressure and better still, does not pass on the pressures down the line. A good manager is a shock absorber!

Honesty – even at times when it is uncomfortable
This is perhaps the single biggest casualty in corporate life! We are seeing increasing levels of dishonesty and corruption in corporate circles.

I have routinely heard about university placement officers bribing corporate managers to hire people from their campuses.

When a manager is dishonest or even remains silent while coming across acts of omission, he is in effect committing a grave mistake! To stand up for what is right and speak up even when it is uncomfortable, makes for a great person that people will admire.

CHAPTER TEN

Trust

In his book, *Seven Habits of Highly Effective People*, Stephen Covey says this, "Trust is the glue of life. It's the most essential ingredient in effective communication. It's the foundational principle that holds all relationships."

We don't need much convincing on the importance of trust in human relationships. It is the basis on which love, friendship, and teamwork are built. We've seen it numerous times in our own lives. How a breach of trust rocks relationships irreparably. We know that being trustworthy is half the battle won in any personal or professional negotiation.

With trust also comes credibility. However, sometimes the process is reversed and credibility comes first. If you work under a manager who has a record of running a Fortune 500 company, you will trust him implicitly, at least to begin with. On the other hand, if your manager is a good friend, a good man, a trustworthy man, his business decisions will carry a lot of credibility with you.

So we can think of both these core values as complements. What comes first is not as important as it is to realize that they breathe life into one another, that they grow together.

In this chapter, we will look at some of the impediments to trust that we must all encounter in the workplace. After all, we all know that we should look after the bond of trust that we build with our fellow beings, and yet at various times, many of us make choices that jeopardize it.

Why?

The short answer is that there are always competing factors that tempt us away from being trustworthy. Betrayal is okay, we tell ourselves, if the person doesn't know that he or she is being betrayed. We trust ourselves, ironically, to get away with it, to sweep it under the carpet. The world is always offering us incentives to betray, to be disloyal, and though we resist these calls of the devil most times, eventually we succumb.

And the trust we build over days, months, and years is gone in a moment.

All of this applies to just about any situation in our life—both personal and professional—but let's spend some more time discussing this fuzzy concept of trust.

In situations, when we go travelling, perhaps, or when we meet someone on the bus with whom we know we won't interact on a regular basis, the temptation to defect is larger. The rewards for defecting are larger. We don't have to be nice, because we know that this relationship is going to be a short one. We don't have to be polite to the beggar on the street, because you see him today and you don't see him tomorrow. But if it's your boss, or even your colleague, since you will be building a long-term relationship with her, it pays to be polite, to be nice, and to cooperate.

This is probably why employees almost transform into strangers once they resign from their place of work. They become more problematic, less committed, and altogether nastier to deal with. The more cynical among us will say that the *true person has emerged*, but I would suggest that there is no such thing as a *true person*. It's just that we behave differently in short-term versus long-term situations. Being nice is a better long-term strategy. Being nasty is a better short-term strategy.

Only when we convince ourselves that a given transaction is a one-off encounter will we give in to the temptation of betraying. If we convince ourselves that every chance meeting is the first of many, then we will automatically train ourselves to be nicer and to be more trusting.

You know that the elderly lady, to whom you did not give your seat on the bus this morning will never see you again, will probably not even remember your face. You know that the person you met at the sales conference in Goa and chatted with for a few minutes will probably struggle to recall the meeting a few days down the line. You know that the parking lot assistant you yelled at in the basement of a shopping mall last night will never come face to face with you elsewhere or again. Therefore, you let go of yourself a little. You don't hold yourself down to the same exacting moral standard that you follow with people you know and need to transact on a more regular basis like your neighbors, friends, and colleagues. Even the people you don't like, but tolerate.

So far, we've seen how our behaviors change between short-term transactions and long-term relationships. In the remainder of this chapter, we will confine ourselves to behavior in teams, and how to build and sustain trust among groups of people. More specifically, we will look at the basic impediments to trust that all of us face in our professional lives. We will also look at steps to overcome these obstacles, and finally we will ask ourselves what we must do as leaders and managers to build an aura of trust and credibility around us.

Operational Impediments to Trust

One of the main barriers to establishing trust between a manager and his wards is the operational atmosphere in which the company functions. In most workplaces, managers get some instructions from the management above, which are non-negotiable. They are to be passed down to the team members without question or argument.

Examples for these could be quarterly revenue targets, delivery deadlines, the number of promotions that can be given out per quarter, the minimum number of people you *have to have* in your team, etc.

In some of these cases, the manager is not allowed to disclose the actual numbers to her team, but she's instructed to motivate them to achieve the goals nonetheless. This leads to a situation where the employees are not sure what they're working for, and the manager is reluctant to share with them the real details and targets.

As a result, many team meetings descend into banal concepts such as commitment and honesty, which the manager demands (or sometimes requests) but never gives. While these are unavoidable barriers in modern day businesses, we must find ways to manage them better. For instance, an open policy of target sharing could be implemented, whereby a manager shares all her targets and goals with her team members.

Communication and frankness will make this process much easier than it is currently. When targets and goals are set out in the open and discussed freely, employees will be less liable to think that the manager is hiding something from them.

Cultural Impediments to Trust

If operational impediments come from above or elsewhere, cultural barriers to trust building often come from within us. The terminology of traditional management—where you refer to your employees as a subordinate and they refer to you as their superiors—fosters fear among the managed and a sense of power in the manager.

We may not believe in these concepts consciously, and may vociferously deny them. However, the words we use build images in our minds. Moreover, words such as superior and subordinate do nothing but set up images of hierarchy in our heads. As long as we use such words in daily parlance, can we ever hope for a manager to treat his employee as his equal?

The majority of the cultural barriers to trust come from the all too human trait that we possess of deriving status from our titles and possessions. For each of us, there is a list of things that we derive our identities from. For instance, a retired colonel may take a lot of pride in his war medals. A writer may be terribly attached to his books. An entrepreneur may derive much of his identity from the performance of his organization. A mother may attach her sense of status from the achievements of her children. And so on.

I've tried to make a list of different kinds of status illusions. They're necessarily generic and are meant to just give you an idea of what I mean. I'm certain that with some thought, you can come up with a list of your own that applies to you.

- **Status derived from age and experience.** I used to have an uncle—a retired army major—who often said in intense arguments, "How dare you speak to me like that? You should at least respect my age!" Though I am picking on him here, many of us are caught up in this illusion that our age and experiences make us wiser. Though it is true that experience teaches you wisdom, it only teaches you wisdom in the things that you have experienced. Being a teacher for forty years is not going to make you much wiser than a college dropout in matters related to aeronautics, for instance.

- **Status derived from title.** Human beings love to classify things. The first thing you get on securing a job with a company is a title. Even though in our hearts we know that the title says less than it pretends to say, we derive some status from it. And if the word manager is present in our job description, we assume that we're one of the leaders. We wear that badge on our chests. We tell people. We take pride in it.
- **Status derived from education.** In India, there is a huge premium on which educational institution you graduated from. Colleges such as the IIT, IIM, and ISB are talked about in reverential whispers, and graduates from these places are treated like gold dust. Is it surprising, then, that people derive a lot of status from their degrees and colleges? An MBA graduate, for instance, will feel entitled to a managerial role, and will resent working under a person who is less qualified than he is.
- **Status derived from pay check.** Organizations go through a lot of pain to prevent employees from discussing their salaries for this very reason. There is no easier way to fan the flame of envy, than to bring up the subject of how much each

person is getting paid. Person A, who earns more than Person B, feels that he's more important to the organization, and he will resist working effectively under someone who earns lesser than he does.

We will take up some of these status illusions, and look at the steps that we can take as managers to mitigate these effects. We cannot make them go away, but we can and should rein in their damage as much as we can.

Cultural Impediments to Trust:

Connections

In several hierarchical organizations, the old timers, regardless of their position in the company, draw their sense of status from knowing the *higher-ups*. I know of several organizations where employees have direct access to the Chairman or Vice-Chairman and enjoy their confidence. The top management also tends to encourage this channel in order to ensure that they get to hear of all of the on-goings at different levels in the organization.

Professional managers in the system are helpless in this situation and tend to accept this practice and look the other way.

Thus, a special status is conferred on the select few.

Titles/Designations

Titles and designations are a big deal in India. People carry their designations and titles to all social events like parties, get-togethers, and weddings. It is not uncommon to hear people whispering stuff like "He is the MD of Xyz Company, He is the general manager/bank manager/IAS Officer, etc. "I happened to come across one designation on a visiting card, which read *General Manager-cum-Vice President* and when I asked the owner of the card what it meant he shrugged his shoulders and said, "I don't really know but it looks good on my card!"

The word manager confers social status and even improves the prospects in the matrimonial market.

One company launched a major initiative to make designations creative and exciting and came out with designations like *Chief Fun Officer, Chief Enthusiasm Officer*, etc. One of the senior managers walked up to the HR team and asked if he could keep his old designation (the mainstream one) until his daughter's wedding gets fixed!

Status from English Speaking

The convent educated English speaking class versus the vernacular educated class is another deep divide. Many engineers who join the workforce come from vernacular backgrounds, struggle to rub shoulders with the urbanized folks. As a result, they feel inferior, don't speak up, and tend to lose out on several opportunities to get ahead in their careers.

Status from Higher Education

Today, a bachelor's degree is considered the very minimum to enter the job market. From there on, of course, you have the education hierarchy with engineers and doctors occupying the top slots in society.

Families are willing to buy medical seats by paying big bucks toward a *capitation fee* (another word for bribe) as high as two crores for a medical seat. For a boy, this is an investment with an ROI in the matrimonial market!

In recent years, the obsession with IIT/IIM/ISB has touched feverish heights. The coaching /tutorial market for preparing students for CAT/JEE are worth several lakh crores given the absolute madness among aspirants to clinch a place in IIT/IIM. This is seen as the ultimate passport for success.

Employers and venture capitalists further fuel this craze by queuing up to hire IIT/IIM graduates as the ultimate super heroes!

A recent study revealed that 96 percent of all startups funded in the last few years had either an IIT or IIM founder/co-founder or better still the IIT+IIM combination.

Social Impediments to Trust

Like it or not, the organization you work in is a microcosm of the society in which it exists. The employees are members of that society first before they're workers in the company, and they're people first, before they're your team members. Therefore, all the social structures of the wider society are present in your organization.

In his book, *India After Gandhi*, historian and writer Ramachandra Guha says that Indian society can be divided along five different lines. They are:

- Religion – India is a diverse country with Muslims, Sikhs, Christians, and Hindus living in apparent harmony. Nevertheless, there are constant waves in this sea of unity, and we must expect such conflicts to erupt in the workplace as well.
- Caste – India's dominant religion, Hinduism, is broken up into four main castes and almost twenty sub-castes. Islam, Christianity, and Sikhism have their own sects. Members of one caste disagree with members of the

others in some fundamental ways, so it's only natural that debates and arguments—not to mention fights—arise from time to time.

- Language – India is divided into twenty-nine states, many of which have their own language. Each language has its own script, its own history of literature, and its own culture. They say that if you want to experience culture shock in India, all you have to do is peep into your neighbor's house.
- Economic Class – Traditionally, Indian society consisted of the ruling class and the plebs. More recently, the middle class has emerged, but the difference between the rich and the poor is incredible. India is a land in which the rich get everything and the poor get nothing.
- Gender – Indian society is patriarchal. Gender roles have been sharply defined by society. The mores are changing, though, and this has brought in an active debate between the two genders. As it is to be expected, there is significant friction, and tempers often flare up on both sides.

All these five fault lines will exist in the workplace too, in the teams that you manage. Very often, these five are not mutually exclusive either. A Brahmin may feel superior to a Shudra, but he may also feel inferior to him because the latter is earning more. Moreover, what happens when the Brahmin is a male and the Shudra is a woman? There are many combinations in which these complexes and feelings will emerge, and each one of them will have an impact on how well your team functions.

As manager, it's your job to take all of these differences and somehow fuse them into a coherent whole. It is not necessary that every person in your team should be friends with everyone else. Nevertheless, it is necessary that they learn to work with one another regardless of their personal equations.

Social Impediments to Trust

This takes on different hues:

Religion:
Given the fact that 80 percent of Indians are Hindus by religion, it simply means that most of the workforce is Hindu by religion. But not withstanding this dominance, one still finds several organizations who would have an unspoken rule that they would only hire or prefer to hire people from a particular religion.

Particularly in South India, it is not uncommon to find traditional, conservative organizations founded by Hindus that do not hire Christians and Muslims.

Likewise, there are Christian/Muslim founded organizations that would hire their own fraternity.

I have also seen in some cases, where the Head of the department belongs to a particular religion or caste and he/she would tend to hire people from the same background. A leading BPO HR Head for example, happens to be a Christian and it is no accident that all key positions in his department, are held by Christians that perhaps even belong to the same Church!

Language/Region:
Again, this bias for language is very evident at all levels. If the Project Head speaks a certain language, one tends to see more of the same in the team!

The minority employees who don't speak the language of the boss tend to be left out when team members break into their mother tongue!

Gender:
The fact that India is a patriarchal society is well known. Even with the advancement of education and more women coming into the workforce, the gender bias toward males remains obscenely high.

In the worst of cases like in manufacturing, the women representation can be as low as 10 percent and in the mid and senior levels it can often be zero as I have seen. In the best of cases like IT, things look better at 30 percent in many companies like Infosys, Cognizant, Mindtree.

At the higher levels, the presence of women managers and leaders is conspicuous by their absence.

The Indian male is threatened and still cannot accept a woman peer or a woman boss.

India is losing out a critical part of its workforce by grossly neglecting and sidelining women. In my organization, things are different. Sixty percent of our team members are women and we have seen the difference that they make!

Conclusion

- In this chapter, we've examined the question of trust. We tried to look into some of the reasons as to why we find it difficult to build and maintain relationships of trust.
- The way to overcome operational impediments is to open up communication channels. Managers and team members should discuss their respective goals in a frank, forthright manner, which will eliminate the culture of fear.
- With cultural impediments, the trick is to accept them. Investing in personal development and mastery sessions—both for

the managers and for the managed—will prove to be useful in the long run.

- The strategy with social impediments is also to first acknowledge them publicly within the team. The longer you spend hoping that they will not rear their ugly heads, the longer you're sitting on a time bomb. Individual mentoring sessions, reading recommendations, and team building activities will help alleviate (but not eliminate) social differences.

CHAPTER ELEVEN

Credibility

Credibility comes from the Latin word *credo*, which means *to believe*. Simply put, a manager with credibility commands attention and focus from his team members. Every so often, you come across a leader for whom his team is willing to walk through a wall. That kind of credibility doesn't come naturally. It has to be created. Just like integrity and trust, much of the credibility that you will carry with your team is a reflection of your inner self. Modify your inner self enough and it will reap rewards on its own.

I will highlight some of the important things that serve to build credibility in a leader. Again, I will try my best to embellish each theoretical point with examples from my own past. Occasionally I will use examples that I have read about or observed from a neutral standpoint.

Develop Expertise

If you're the best developer in a team of developers, they will automatically look to you for direction. In a cricket team, the best batsman or the best bowler is generally first in line when it comes to consideration for captaincy. If you wish to gain credibility in the eyes of your team, the most important thing to do would be to increase your knowledge in your domain and on the team's activities.

One of the most common gripes of technical teams working under a manger is that the manager does not know anything. Don't give them that excuse. Show them that your expertise is no less than theirs is, and you will automatically get their attention.

Develop Expertise: My Experience

For anyone to establish credibility today, it is important to demonstrate expertise. In the knowledge economy populated by knowledge workers, the leader must know his/her stuff.

I am reminded of a terrible phase in my life when I came close to bankruptcy. In a desperate bid to make some quick money, I ventured into the field of energy conservation. The opportunity tempted me with huge profits and the magical short cut to financial success (which clearly does not exist!).

I didn't know a thing about electrical energy and I depended on other people to get things done. I didn't have a clue as to whether things were working out or not. I had no way to find out until I ran out of money and had to shut shop, adding to my losses.

That day, I decided that I would never ever venture into an area where I did not have reasonable core competence.

Since then, I have stuck to my core competencies and managed to get back on track. There is no substitute for building expertise to build credibility.

Accountability

Teams love leaders that take all the blame and disperse all the credit. The great leaders of the world have a way of absorbing all the criticism when things are not going well and dispersing all the good feedback when things are going well.

Actions Speak Louder Than Words

Do not ask your team members to do anything that you wouldn't do yourself. Organizations are full of managers that request their teams to work on weekends while they themselves take the day off. Even if the manager has nothing to do, if his team is coming in on a Sunday, it is his duty to come in as well, even if it's just to show that he's there for them whenever they need him.

Professionalism and Stoicism

One of the most essential points of leaders who command respect and loyalty from their team members is that they're stoic to both failure and success. For better or worse, being an emotional leader will give the message to people looking up to you that you do not have it under control. Giving off an aura of self-control and good humor—especially in times of high stress—will send out the message that everything is under control.

A great leader is one who takes the blame for any mistakes by the team and passes on all credit when the team succeeds. The most famous anecdote for this is attributed to Abdul Kalam's boss Satish Dhawan when they were boss and subordinate in ISRO. This story of the failure of India's first satellite is well known, although Abdul Kalam was the Project Head, Satish Dhawan, the Head of ISRO took all the blame for its failure. When the satellite was successfully re-launched a year later, Satish Dhawan passed on all the credit to Abdul Kalam and his team. This is the true hallmark of a great leader.

CHAPTER TWELVE

Transparency

The word *transparency* is abused in management circles. Often it is used synonymously with trust. However, it is worth mentioning that even in the most trusting relationships—both personal and professional—transparency can be missing. A certain amount of transparency helps build trust in a relationship.

If we have to define this, we can do so by saying that two parties are transparent with one another if they communicate their relative objectives and motivations clearly, openly and frankly. Often in a business climate, a certain amount of secrecy is necessary—many cards ought to be played while being kept close to the chest—so people proceed to build walls all around themselves, alienating everybody in their teams.

Once when I asked a manager why his employees were not given a certain piece of information, which was the bigger picture of the project, he responded by saying, "Why do they need to know?" What he did not say but implied with his tone of voice were the words—it is none of their business.

Such managers, who are reluctant to open the lines of communication with their teams, often unwittingly hinder the progress of their projects. When taken to an extreme, such managers often end up being toxic, and the culture of opacity flows down to the team members. Each individual team member in such a team builds mini fortresses around herself, and before you know it, nobody in the team is talking to anybody else, and everyone is playing a game of hard-nosed poker.

The focus shifts from pulling together to achieve a common goal to playing our individual cards right to reach our individual goals. Team members often look at their colleagues as competitors rather than trustees and friends.

Going back to the topic of toxicity, here is an example of a typical toxic manager. To begin with, he is full of himself. The only reason he has risen through the ranks is seniority. He has worked in the same team for more than eight years, which automatically got him promoted to the position of team leader. It is clearly not because of merit, capability, or competency. In recent years when Gen Y and Gen Z professionals—highly talented and knowledgeable—are entering the workforce, he is threatened by these competent youngsters; and he shows it out through micromanagement.

Now, he did not become team leader only because of seniority, he is also very good at keeping his boss happy. Essentially, he is a *Yes boss* person who kowtows to the boss. Being extremely bureaucratic, he enjoys throwing the rulebook at people at every opportunity. However, he does have favorites and tends to be partial toward them. He typically makes life difficult for people who threaten his position, and attempts to outsmart him. You may wonder how these kinds of managers survive in workplaces. It is because he has somehow managed to surpass his own boss and get into the good books of his CEO.

Although he manages to keep his superiors happy, he disallows people under him from growing. He decides who gets which project, who is recognized, who gets an increment etc. He exerts complete control over management and decision-making. He willfully goes about destroying people's careers and oppressively keeps people under his thumb. With workplaces being restructured, and more organizations adopting a flat structure, it is getting difficult for these managers to survive. Nevertheless, you can always find toxic managers like him in certain pockets in all industries.

Reasons for Toxicity

There are two broad reasons for toxicity—outward and inward. Outward reasons include things that are outside our locus of control. These can be organizational metrics, performance, revenue, and profit targets, pre-defined KPIs, bad history between team members, etc.

Often these are not the result of the manager's doing, but if the manager does not take steps to correct the course of the train as soon as he discovers that something is wrong, all he will do is drive it straight into a wreck. And by then it will be too late.

Inward reasons for toxicity emerge from character traits the manager possesses. Some of us are not natural communicators, and even in our personal relationships, we rely more on unspoken gestures and body language to get messages across. While this is not necessarily a bad thing, in a professional set up, talking about issues often trumps waiting for people to pick up on visual cues.

Also, the manager may be going through personal strife of her own. This may lead to her being preoccupied by other events in her life during working hours. She may act out of character, and therefore let things in the team slip.

The most common source of inborn toxicity is simply misinformation. Most managers of today have learnt traditional management strategies from their mentors and from textbooks. Therefore, most of them are focused overtly on results and the intangible elements of management such as communication gets waylaid in the race for an extra percentage point of revenue. The solution in this case is to undergo personal change and unlearn the things that we've learnt in a different world and a different time.

The most important trait that a manager must develop is to be nimble, to understand that what worked yesterday may not work today. What works today may not work tomorrow. So the aspiring manager must always be willing to learn, to observe, and to experiment to suit her style with the environment in which she finds herself.

Having said this, there are concrete steps that a manager can take to establish a culture of transparency in her team. In the remainder of this chapter, we will look into these three aspects. Where possible, I will embellish my recommendations with real life examples.

First Step to Transparency: Goal Setting

In my experience, every big company in the country has a certain period at the beginning of the financial year, set aside for goal setting. This is when employees trudge into their manager's office and communicate to her their goals for the year. The manager—in theory at least—reviews the employee's proposals and works with them to create a measurable set of parameters by which judgment can be passed at the end of the year.

In practice, this is all a farce.

Employees look at this task as a chore. I've conducted interviews with some experienced people in big organizations, and more than 90 percent of them reacted with disinterest when I mentioned the word goal setting. Many have no idea what to put in their target documents. Most treat the whole process with a healthy amount of skepticism, sometimes stating flatly that none of it matters.

Managers, for their part, are happy to push the ball gently into employees' courts. "If they don't care about their own goals," they say, "what can we do?"

Therefore, we have a ridiculous exercise that takes place for a good month or so every year in every organization, and most of the people participating in it simply don't care. Is it any wonder, then, that there is a significant amount of discontent between employee and manager when the time comes for pay hikes and promotions? If we falter on the first step, how can we hope to make our journey a peaceful one?

I'm going to put the responsibility of communicating the importance of goal setting squarely on the shoulders of the manager. If your team is disinterested or disengaged with the process of setting their goals, then I would suggest that it's because you haven't done a good enough job of telling them why they should care.

After all, that is why you're the manager. That is why you're the leader. If your team members were all cock-a-hoop to begin with and can't wait to cut their teeth into the work they've been given, whatever is the need for you?

The blueprint for goal setting, then, should follow roughly the following steps:

1. Communicate the importance of setting measurable goals to every employee in your team. This can take the form of a *carrot* or the *stick*, but my experience is that a *carrot* always works best. Tell them that their hikes and their promotions will be fully aligned to whether or not they achieve their goals. If they don't believe you, then you have a trust issue. You may have to earn their trust first.
2. Clearly document measurable goals in close consultation with the employee. There will be significant back and forth discussions at this stage, with most employees pushing for the bar to be lowered and with most managers pulling it a few rungs higher. Split these goals into three parts.
3. First, agree on the *lower bar* of minimum achievable goals. These are goals that an employee—given his experience and ability—has to achieve. This is commonly known in the industry as hygiene factor. The employee will not get rewarded for achieving this lower bar, but he will be punished for not achieving it. Discuss with the employee the complete repercussions of not achieving this level. If you need to tell him that he will be demoted if he doesn't achieve these goals, do so right now. Don't wait until the performance appraisal time to break the bad news.

4. Second, agree on a *higher bar* of goals, which represent the employee's next role in his career path. These are goals that the employee is not expected to reach, and is not within his brief to attempt. So if he achieves these goals, it means that he has gone over and above his call of duty, and is therefore to be rewarded. Discuss all the rewards that the employee could expect to receive if he reaches this bar. Once again, be frank and open. Reveal all.
5. Third, communicate to the employee the consequences of being between the two bars, in the *band of adequate performance*. Here, the rewards to the employee will be based on the discretion of the manager. This is the part that most employees don't understand. There is a band in which rewards cannot be concretely defined and have to be given out based on the discretion of the manager. If possible, agree upon a set of parameters based on which your decision will be based. This is to ensure that your employee will not be taken by surprise come end of the year.
6. After agreeing upon goals and bands, ask the employee what you can do as manager to enable him to achieve his goals. This is an important step because it tells your employee that both of you are working on the same side, and more importantly, that you want him

to succeed, that you're willing to make things happen in order to help him succeed.
7. Finally, set aside a certain part of the year—one month is often more than enough—to prepare the employee for his future role in his career path. Discussions should of course be had with the employee on what his chosen path is, and what kind of roles he would like to be trained in. This strategy has many benefits, not the least of which is that you will constantly up-skill your team members. Your team will also look up to you as a mentor, because you're not only taking interest in their current work but also in their long-term careers.

Performance appraisals are highly subjective. They are mostly done on the whims and fancies of the bosses. It is rarely scientific and objective. This causes ambiguity in organizations because many times, employees are under the impression that they are doing well. This notion is encouraged by their bosses who consistently say that they are doing well and that things are on track. However, during appraisals, employees are shocked because they are told that they have just met expectations. This confuses them because they have slogged and as per their boss's verbal reviews too, they have done well. Thus, they do not understand why they have not exceeded expectations. The main reason is that goals and their measurements have not been put in place. And this is extremely important for performance appraisals.

In order to avoid this ambiguity and confusion, performance metrics should be clearly articulated. I believe each employee must be given at least five or six key result areas (KRAs) that he or he must accomplish through the year with measurable results. Of course, in sales, such KRAs are more easily accomplished than in departments like human resources (HR) or learning and development (L&D), but it is not impossible.

For instance, an HR executive can be given the following goal, "The employee satisfaction score is currently 3.8 on a 5-point scale. Now, you will be part of a team that is responsible for improving the employee satisfaction score to at least 4 on a 5-point scale. I need you to outline three specific things you are going to do to improve these scores." In this example, the HR executive has been given a goal along with achievable metrics attached to it. Let's look at another example for someone from the L&D department. "You are responsible for the first time manager program and you must ensure that 80 percent of the first time manager population is covered in this program. That means 80 percent of the first time managers must undergo this program." This becomes her first metric. Her next metric can relate to the effectiveness of the program.

"Participants must evaluate all the programs that you are in charge of at a minimum of 4.5 on a 5-point scale in terms of program satisfaction."

Now, when someone is given such clear goals and metrics, confusion and ambiguity decreases. The problem is that clear goals and metrics are rarely provided. Most employees have to make do with the roles provided in their job descriptions. Inevitably, an employee feels that she is satisfying all her roles and responsibilities as stated to her but then her manager says, "Oh, you missed this or you did not get 80 percent of the first time managers on board." If the metrics were not provided to her, how would she know that she had to get 80 percent of them on board?

At either the beginning or the last quarter of the year, every manager must have a conversation with her team member encouraging him or her to come up with goals for the year. She can discuss each member's goals along with the goals that she has set for him or her to arrive at a set number of goals to be achieved. According to me, each employee must not have more than five or six KRAs.

When it comes to performance appraisals, at the junior level, objectivity should ideally constitute 80 percent of the appraisal. The remaining 20 percent can include the manager's judgment of each of her team members. If an employee gets a met expectation review and the manager is able to produce data showing his or her goals and metrics that were not achieved, there would be no doubt or discussion. It would be a perfectly objective performance appraisal and the only thing an employee can do is to plan better and achieve his or her goals before the next appraisal. At mid-management level, the objectivity to subjectivity ratio can be 60:40. Sixty percent can be objective and 40 percent can be subjective because bosses need to look for other attributes at this stage. An employee might be assessed on various soft skills and leadership potential that cannot always be objectively assessed. The takeaway in this section is that when there is too much subjectivity in judging employee performance, there is no transparency. When objectivity is higher, goals are clearer and discussions involve metrics. This results in employees, managers and the organization performing better.

General Electric is a name that is famous in multiple industries. When Jack Welch became chairman of General Electric, he gave all his country managers one clear goal, "We must be either number one or number two in that industry, or we must get out of it." He gave this unambiguous revenue goal to everyone. For instance, if you were the country head of consumer durables in India, you had to be number one or number two in that industry or else shut it down. While it may sound astonishing, this one goal turned around GE during Jack Welch's time. Everyone was clear on what had to be done and this led to GE consolidating many of their business. They shut down industries that were not viable and from about a hundred different industries they brought it down to less than twenty. With this singular goal, GE was able to make history.

Second Step to Transparency: Feed-Forward
(copyright Marshall Goldsmith)

I do believe that words carry images and meanings, and while feedback sounds like something to be afraid of, feed-forward carries a distinct feeling of looking ahead and learning. This word created by Marshall Goldsmith, it doesn't sound like this deep, dark dungeon into which employees go pale with fear and confusion.

The following points should be used as a blueprint for a typical feed-forward mechanism.

1. It should happen at least once a month. The employee should get information on how he's doing, and where he's likely to end up if he works at the same level. For instance, as a manager, you will say, "If you continue working at the same level, in my opinion, you will reach this point by the end of the year" or "If you wish to achieve you upper band of

goals, you will need to improve in these key areas." Or "I think you're running the risk of not achieving your minimum achievable goals. Is everything okay? Can I do something to support you?"

2. The purpose of this exercise is to keep the employee fully informed on how he's performing relative to his goals. The first part of this exercise is to look ahead, at the goals, and track current progress based on what lies in the future.

3. The other part of the process focuses on the past. The manager uses past performance of the employee to give him specific feedback on his improvement areas. Often, framing this discussion as questions works the best, because it allows the employee to open up and discuss. So instead of telling him he needs to work on his presentation skills, you could say, "I've noticed that you're not comfortable making presentations. Would I be right in saying that you find public speaking challenging? "If he says yes, you could ask him further questions like, "Is there any training we can arrange for you to improve that aspect of your work?"

4. The most important thing to remember with feed-forward sessions is to not allow them to become opportunities to speak. Too often in these meetings, the manager talks a lot and

the employee nods a lot. It should be the other way round. If you're doing all the talking in your feed-forward sessions and your employee is staying silent, you may want to consciously tell yourself to ask more questions. And to listen more.

Third Step to Transparency: Performance Appraisal

Is there a phrase that is more feared among employees than *performance appraisal*? I've never met any person—no matter what level he or she was at—who happily made their way into his boss's office at the end of the year. Invariably the feelings that accompany this dreaded time are inadequacy, fear, uncertainty, and ultimately hopelessness.

If we establish the first two steps outlined in this chapter into our teams, none of these negative feelings will accompany the performance appraisal time. Most of the bad blood between managers and their employees arise because a) there is no specific direction to the goal-setting exercise, and b) there is no defined feed-forward loop that keeps the team member informed about his progress.

If these two flaws are corrected, at least the employee will not walk into an appraisal meeting being fearful of the unknown. At least he will know what is coming. At least he will not be taken by surprise, and further have a sense of being betrayed by his manager.

A disgruntled team member at least shows that he cares. But once employees descend into this feeling of apathy then you may have lost them forever. An angry response from an employee is to be feared, but a wry smile and a shrug is more alarming, because that shows resignation. In addition, a resigned employee will never be motivated to work for you.

Yet this is the situation I have encountered in almost all my interviews. There is first a sarcastic smile, then a shrug of the shoulders, and a rolling of the eyes. "It's all pre-decided," they say. "We can't help it. It's all in the manager's hands."

This experience has driven me to dub performance appraisal meetings as corporate torture chambers.

The Need to Move beyond Hikes and Promotions

In my experience of corporate life, performance appraisal meetings are focused only on two things only—a hike in salary and a promotion. Common knowledge dictates that money and fame are humanity's lasting obsessions. It appears that things in the corporate world are no different. An employee walks into an appraisal meeting typically interested in either a raise (i.e. more money) or a better title.

However, as managers, we must move conversations away from these two topics. Both raises and promotions ought to be seen by both parties as consequences of the employee achieving his goals. They're not ends in themselves. Just because someone has spent eight years working in the same role, you're not obligated to promote him. On the other hand, even a greenhorn, if she achieves her goals, should be promoted and rewarded.

The dialogue, therefore, should focus on just two questions:

1. Did the employee reach her slated *lower band* of goals? This is the set of minimum achievable goals that you've documented together at the beginning of the year.
2. Did the employee reach her slated *upper band* of goals? This is the set of *beyond the call of duty* goals that you've documented together at the beginning of the year.

There are only three possible outcomes to these questions. One, the employee has said yes to both questions. Two, she has said yes to the first and no to the second. Three, she has said no to both.

Of course, there should be some debate on whether the employee did indeed perform as well as she says she did. As manager, you should challenge her to provide evidence of all her work, and then assess her work, taking into account, your experiences of working with her throughout the year.

Once this debate is done, the rewards are already laid out in the goal-setting document and will accrue to the employee automatically. There may still be lingering disagreement over where the employee stands—especially in the grey area between the lower and upper bars—but at least she won't accuse you of being furtive and opaque.

Managing Underperformers

In any team you manage, a certain proportion of them will underperform i.e. they will say no to both the questions asked in the previous section. They will fail to reach their lower band of goals and will be classified as inadequate.

Many managers treat underperformers as bad eggs that have to be handled. Like an uncomfortable but benign outgrowth, they just have to be put up with, and managed perfunctorily. Meetings with such employees are generally terse and to the point. Sometimes they're rude. I've heard more than one manager say to me in as many words, "I don't want to waste my time in pulling dead weight."

However, it is my contention that we give up on people as dead weight way too easily. Often, there are legitimate reasons for an employee's underperformance. Very rarely do you find the mythical troublemaker in the team who doesn't listen to anybody and goes about his business without the smallest regard for the team's outcome. Indeed, if I were to be brutally honest, prima donna behavior is more common in star performers than it is in underperformers.

Generally, underperformers display lower self-esteem, possess weaker social skills, have less fun, and make fewer friends than the average team member. They usually have something going on in their personal lives that are preventing them from performing at a level they would like to. Tragically, the typical reaction from managers to such people is not empathy and understanding but ridicule and scorn, which pushes them deeper into their shell.

What is the solution to this, then? My suggestion is to include a personal element to all meetings with all your employees throughout the year. Both during goal-setting and feed-forward sessions, set aside perhaps 10 percent of the meeting's time to personal conversation, where you and your employee just get to know each other better. Find out how many children they have. Where do their spouses work? How many siblings do they have? What is the living situation of their parents? What is their financial life like?

Asking team members these details may make you come across as intrusive. What I do, therefore, is begin by sharing my details to get the conversation going. It's much easier to build a relationship of trust when you make the first move. For instance, look at the following two approaches to a personal conversation.

1. I had such a long weekend. My elder son had football practice in the morning, and the younger one just wouldn't get out of bed. I had to carry him all the way to the ground, and after returning home, he insisted that I sit with him and listen to him play the violin. What about you? What are your children like on weekends?
2. So, how was your weekend? What did you do? Do you go out much with family on weekends?

Put yourself in the shoes of your employee. Which of the above two approaches would elicit a sincere response? And yet, isn't the second option what most people naturally gravitate toward when they wish to begin a conversation?

Finding a common point of interest like kids, spouse, family, movies, music, sports. The list is endless. And then opening the conversation on the specific topic will always make your personal relationships deeper, whether it is with employees, colleagues, your own managers, or with your friends.

Making a habit out of introducing a personal element to each of your meetings has a double advantage. First, it gives you a decent idea of the emotional health of your team member. You will not be taken by surprise if he suddenly tells you that his grandmother is sick and that he has to go away for a few days. Second, it relaxes both of you and allows you to connect on a deeper, human level.

This human connection is what most underperformers crave. If you give it to them, you will go a long way to eliminating all the dead weight from your team.

CHAPTER THIRTEEN

Motivation

In the world of management, motivation is the Holy Grail. If a manager understands what motivates each of his team members, what makes them tick, there's not much that can go wrong in the quest for performance and excellence.

But like the Holy Grail, finding the motivations of people can be a tricky business. We human beings are notoriously adept at hiding our true aspirations, not only from others but also from ourselves. We go through long friendships, relationships, and marriages with people whom we think we know inside and out. And yet, every now and then a certain facet of their personality reveals itself and surprises us.

It is not an easy business knowing what makes people tick.

This is perhaps why most managers in workplaces fall back on the easy, tried and tested technique of assuming that their teams are motivated by the tangibles of money, free lunches, bonuses, and promotions being the most often dangled carrots.

Many companies pay overtime to their employees if they stay back beyond working hours, and if they come in to work on weekends. Some managers give their teams a free rein, in terms of the lunch they can order if they work on a Sunday. Others offer monetary bonuses or gifts. Yet others hint at a promotion or a salary hike being contingent on an employee's performance on a given project.

Do these work? Of course they do. But as we shall see in this chapter, they don't work as well as we think they do.

The Problem with "Tangible" Motivators

Tangible motivators! They're essentially bottomless pits. The more one has, the more one wants. As in our personal lives, we cannot satisfy want for material things by fulfilling it. That thirst is unquenchable.

It's not unlike being on an addictive drug. So if you motivate your employees purely by material rewards, you will find that your team will come to expect more and more rewards in the future, and indeed, they will need it to perform the same amount of work that they used to.

If this sounds too morbid, that is exactly how a consumer culture behaves. India is now taking its first steps toward mass consumerism. Giant billboards of this product or that accost us everywhere we go. The giant industry of advertising works on the principle that consumers should be kept in the constant state of wanting something. Not only is it important to show a need and fulfill it with a product, but it is of paramount importance not to fulfill the need *permanently*.

Someone who is contented with his Onida television will never fork out enough money to buy a Sony Smart TV. So you make him discontented with his current possession first, then show him the features of the new possession, and encourage him to displace it. And then, allow some time to pass and repeat the process.

Advertising taps into our most basic need of wanting material things. And like crack addicts, we need more to get the same kick. After growing up in a two-room house all his life, a friend of mine bought a three-bedroom house in a plush apartment complex. Then he upgraded to a villa. Then he bought a plot of land and built a double storey bungalow on it. Now, he's in negotiation to buy the property next door so that he can annex it to his own.

We see the same thing with money. We think x amount is enough for us to live happily. But once we achieve the x, we find that our lifestyle has already expanded, and that we need more to make us happy. And of course, once we reach our new goal, we find that we need further more.

This is not a criticism of humanity. This is just natural behavior for human beings. We're greedy by nature. We're hoarders by nature. The more we have, the more we want. It is why even in an era of great material abundance of wealth and resources, many of us who have nothing to complain about still find ourselves anxious and depressed.

Our fears are manifold, but as Alain de Botton says in his book, *Status Anxiety*, the biggest motivation for human beings is the love and acceptance of other human beings.

> *Every adult life could be said to be defined by two great love stories. The first - the story of our quest for sexual love is well known and well charted. Its vagaries form the staple of music and literature. It is socially accepted and celebrated. The second - the story of our quest for love from the world is a more secret and shameful tale. If mentioned, it tends to be in caustic, mocking terms, as something of interest chiefly to envious or deficient souls, or else the drive for status is interpreted in an economic sense alone. And yet this second love story is no less intense than the first. It is no less complicated, important, or universal, and its setbacks are no less painful. There is heartbreak here too.*

He says that each one of us seems to have within us an inborn uncertainty about who we really are, and about what our native qualities are. To settle these uncertainties, we turn to the world around us to validate us. And in the course of this validation, we gravitate toward money, because we think that money often buys respect, love, acceptance, sometimes even adoration from our peers.

So it is not really money that we desire. It is the intangible things that we think money will get us. The nature of desire is such that we feel that surmounting our current ambition will lead us to a state of *nirvana*, but we don't remember that once this goal is achieved, we will train our sights on the next goal, along with the anxiety and depression that will bring with it.

In the words of de Botton:

> *We are tempted to believe that certain achievements and possessions will give us enduring satisfaction. We are invited to imagine ourselves scaling the steep cliff face of happiness in order to reach a wide, high plateau on which we will live out the rest of our lives; we are not reminded that soon after gaining the summit, we will be called down again into fresh lowlands of anxiety and desire.*

And hitting close to home about the uncertainties and fears that most employees get crushed under, he says:

> *The travails of being an employee include not only uncertainty about the duration of one's employment, but also the humiliation of many working practices and dynamics. With most businesses shaped like pyramids, in which a wide base of employees gives way to a narrow tip of managers, the question of who will be rewarded—and who left behind—*

typically develops into one of the most oppressive of the workplace, and one which, like all anxieties, feeds off uncertainty. Because achievement in most fields is difficult to monitor reliably, the path to promotion or its opposite can acquire an apparently haphazard connection to results. The successful alpinist of organizational pyramids may not be the best at their jobs, but those who have best mastered a range of dark political arts in which civilized life does not usually offer instruction.

The solution to this is not to stop ourselves or our employees from desiring but to change the focus of their desires by understanding them better. We don't necessarily want money. We want money because we see it as a vehicle to get us the things that we really crave for like respect, status, and appreciation.

De Botton puts the final nail in the coffin of material desires and how they lead us to misery by constantly raising our expectations. Happiness, he says, echoing the thoughts of the Genevan philosopher Jean-Jacques Rousseau, is entirely dependent on our expectations and our desires. He says, "We may be happy with little when we have come to expect little. And we may be miserable with much when we have been taught to expect everything."

Here is a real incident of a company's disastrous attempt to woo their employees with "tangible" motivators that back fired big time!

A Lesson of a Lifetime: narrated by the HR manager himself!

I worked for a garment manufacturing organization that had an operator workforce of 1800 per shift (mostly women). The shift timings were:

1st shift: 6 a.m. to 2 p.m.
2nd shift: between 2 p.m. and 10 p.m.

Absenteeism was hovering around 5 percent, and it was decided that we should work toward 0 percent absenteeism for a week in any one shift. We took the 1st shift as the sample shift and started preparing for the success of this initiative. As a preparatory step, meetings were held with the production team, vendor management team, etc. It was decided that we should try it in the first week of September. Accordingly, all efforts were directed toward this initiative and communication toward this was sent to all operators and supervisors including the transport authorities and canteen contractor.

The project was launched and to our great joy and delight we achieved 100 percent attendance on Monday, Tuesday, and Wednesday. Tense moments followed as even if one person fails to turn up, or if one person comes late or misses the vehicle, the project is a failure. So more efforts were put in to clinch success in the remaining three days of the week.

On Thursday and Friday as well we achieved 100 percent attendance. Come Saturday, we were creating history.

There was so much pressure to ensure that all turn up for work on time on Saturday. The GM, the Financial Controller, and I, as Head of HR, were all in the factory at 5 a.m. to ensure that all vans and buses rolled in on time and tea and snacks were served on time, so that the machines start humming at 6 a.m. to meet the output target for the day.

As luck would have it, everything happened as planned, and we had every employee punch the card on time. The project was a huge success.

Joy filled the place and huge celebrations followed on the floor and factory.

To recognize this amazing milestone, the management wanted to reward the employees. So it was decided that all employees of the first shift who were part of creating history will be recognized during the *Ayudha Pooja* celebration the following month. After a few rounds of discussion, it was decided that all employees would receive a stainless steel utensil. Come *Ayudha Pooja*, we had the usual celebration and at the end of it, a well gift wrapped, stainless steel utensil was given to every employee who was part of this great project. At the end of all the celebration, the works committee members along with a group of senior employees came to us and thanked us for the recognition. They appeared very happy and delighted. Finally, my Financial Controller and I along with the General Manager were relaxing over a cup of tea and cherishing the success.

Suddenly a group of twenty odd operators came to us and voiced their unhappiness over the *Ayudha Pooja* events. Quite surprised at their tone, as Head of HR, I took them to the conference hall to discuss what could have made them happier.

They said
"Sir, we were walking out of the factory when we met a few of the operators working in the second shift coming into the factory. They asked us how the *Pooja* celebration went and what the reward that we got was. We showed them the stainless steel utensil you had given us. They laughed at us and said, "For an achievement that great, you have all got only a *chatie* (a pot in Tamil), eh?" And they did not stop with that ridicule. Some of the operators also said, "Tomorrow when we come into the factory, all of you can sit in a row outside with this *chatie*, and we shall drop some coins in them for you...ha haha!" "Sir, we are very unhappy with this *chatie* that you have given us." I literally fell out of my chair as I heard this. I then went on to ask them what would have made them

happy. The reply they gave me was a lifetime lesson to me.

They said, Sir:

1. A photograph taken with the GM at the centre and you and Financial Controller on either side with all of us would have made us happy. It could have been laminated and hung on the canteen wall in our premises because a lot of visitors would see this photo and know that we created history in this factory. It would have been an inspiring story to tell the others, so they can achieve the same.
2. Also, if a nicely laminated and framed certificate signed by the GM was given to us, we would have placed it on top of the refrigerator, TV, or hung it on a wall at home. We would have shown this to all our friends and relatives visiting our home with so much pride and self-esteem.
3. A small article on this achievement, written and circulated across all factories around the world, would have made us famous in no time. That would have made us feel proud.

I then realized the difference between "tangible" and "intangible" motivators. What I thought will make them happy was extrinsic in nature and the value of it lasted only for twenty minutes. What they were looking for from me was intrinsic in nature.

The eye opener for me was the realization that it would have cost me far less had I given them what they wanted than the lakhs I had spent on buying hundreds of stainless steel utensils—the tangible motivator that ended up in the dustbin!

CHAPTER FOURTEEN

Delegation

An old saying goes *if you can't lead or follow, at least get out of the way*. In the modern world of specialization, much of being a leader is knowing when to get out of the way. If I were to be asked, what is the single most important attribute of a leader? I would suggest that it is her ability to delegate and allows the specialists to express themselves through their work and talent.

Effective delegation is not possible without trust. Most managers think of delegation as an informative exercise, where they tell their wards what is to be done. In this chapter we will see why this is a flawed tactic, why a good delegator not only informs but also inspires his team. Not only does he tell his employees what needs to be done, he also makes it clear why it needs to be done and how it has been done before in other teams and organizations.

Seen this way, delegation is not just a one-time activity that the leader engages in and then steps aside. It's a deeply involved and on-going activity, where progress has to be monitored on a regular basis and re-delegation needs to be done if and when necessary.

Current Status of Delegation

Most often, the Indian manager of today is a poor delegator. There are many reasons for this. We can posit three different areas in which these reasons fall.

1. **Personal reasons**

    One of the biggest human fears is of being redundant. Managers suffer from this quite acutely because a typical manager in an Indian setting relaxes professionally and doesn't re-invent himself. He sees the managerial role as a consequence of being the highest achieving member of the team. He forgets that it is also a stepping stone in his long-term career.

So not only does he have the feelings like "I know better/best" but also has the fear that someone else will take his job if he allows anyone to encroach upon his territory. This is not at all uncommon in a team setting where people who hold knowledge and experience can be seen jealously guarding their intellectual capital without sharing it with others. While this is understandable behavior, this is no way for a leader to perform. A leader should constantly re-invent himself and encourage an atmosphere of sharing and collaborating within his team.

2. Cultural reasons

We've touched upon the cultural aspects of being a manager in earlier chapters. The joint family system that our country is famous for is also responsible for our hierarchical way of thinking. We think of people with age and status to be superior, and we've traditionally been a culture, which places great emphasis on knowledge and imparters of knowledge.

So a manager who climbs to the top of his team by virtue of his perceived superiority over others will find it difficult to give it up. He will look at himself as a guru and the others as shishyas, and in his mind, he will imagine himself leading them. Therefore, he must perform all important tasks himself. He must stay in control always. He must stay on top of everything. In such a cultural environment, it is no surprise that trust and delegation are rarely found.

3. Interpersonal issues

Psychologists have done many studies on the extension of self. Without going into technicalities, we have known for a long time now that at the very base of human attachments like love and friendship, there is this concept where the object of attachment becomes a part of who we are. Once we extend our selves to include that object, we can no longer view it objectively, just as we cannot view ourselves objectively.

Therefore, criticism of the object becomes criticism of self, and we react personally. Studies have shown that these objects of attachment can be anything, from people and pets to something as abstract as ideas and concepts. Once we take ownership of something (i.e. my husband, my dog, my project), something clicks in our minds which makes us incapable of letting them go. The stronger the bond, the harder it is let go and to place the piece of work in someone else's hands.

This is also why we tend to end up hurting those that we love the most, because often we don't think of what is good for them, but what is good for us. Stories of parents imposing their will on their children are not new, and I'm certain that you can think of some from your own life, both with you on the giving and receiving ends of such treatment. In work, a manager who derives his identity from his work and is emotionally wedded to it will find it difficult to think of what is good for the project, and will find himself confusing his own preferences with that of the project.

Delegating Effectively

The primary stated goal of most organizations in the current business world is to ensure that all their employees are working at one level above their current role. This is a common point of conversation during performance appraisal meetings. It is a rare meeting where the manager does not say something like, "Miss X, we need to make sure that you're operating at a level above your current role."

However, for much of the time this is just lip service. The same manager who wants Miss X to work above her station will not find it within himself to trust her with tasks that she must do in order to fulfill that expectation. He will not delegate. In fact, he will be so eager to do everything himself that he will perform some of Miss X's tasks himself, either literally or by proxy (by guiding her with intimate detail about the steps she must take).

As a result, Miss X will in fact perform at a level *below* her current role.

In reality, this is the norm for almost every organization I have had the opportunity to work with. Management says in all their official communication that they want people to take more responsibility, work above their roles, go beyond the call of duty, etc. And yet, in practice, you find that almost every employee in the company is working at a level below their current role.

Why does this happen? The answer is simple: a failure to delegate effectively.

The Problem with Delegating Tasks

Am I saying that delegating doesn't happen at all, or that managers do all the work of their teams by themselves? Not at all. Even a super manager cannot summon up the time needed to complete all of his team's tasks. He does delegate, but I believe not in an effective manner, which displays trust in his employees.

For instance, a common technique of delegation—one that I am sure you will recognize—is to tell the employee exactly *what* he or she must do. The manager, therefore, does not waste time in telling his ward what the overall project's aims are, or what the team is trying to achieve, or what results they wish to see at the end, or anything of this sort. All he will do is call the employee into his cabin and say, "Miss X, please do this, this, and this, and I want it by tomorrow evening."

This is what I call delegating tasks. As task delegating manager, you look at your team members as just resources and dumb robots that cannot be trusted to understand the bigger picture. You think of them as glorified computers, into which a set of tasks are relied upon to complete.

A better way of approaching this business of delegation, I think, is to let your employees in on the conversation of what the team is hoping to achieve. And more importantly, how about communicating to them clearly the results that the project is looking for? That way, you will straight away give them the parameters on which they will be judged, and you will also have come across as being trusting.

So communicate the desired results, perhaps give them the benefit of your experience by telling them how such projects have been implemented in the past, and then leave your employees to figure out their own way. Trust them, be available in a support capacity, and just get out of the way.

Or rather, think of yourself as getting a head start and clearing the path ahead for the rest of your team to follow.

On Strengths and Weaknesses

One of the great foibles of the human race is our obsession with the negative. A symphony that is perfect could be ruined by one false note. A movie with one bad actor could become bad in our eyes. A school student who always comes second in class is bound to get multiple remarks on his report card from his teachers saying that he can come first. In the paths we take in our lives, no matter what they are, we have both thorns and roses, but many of us are inexorably drawn toward the thorns.

Social psychologists have studied this phenomenon, and study after study has shown that we spend more resources on thinking about our negative aspects, or weaknesses, rather than on improving our positive aspects or strengths.

Modern management literature is slowly taking this on board. Some organizations that I know have made a conscious attempt to focus on strengthening their employees' natural strengths instead of spending inordinate amounts of time working on their weaknesses. Performance appraisals in these companies are more strength oriented rather than what the employee needs to work on.

This doesn't mean that weaknesses are not touched upon at all. Some weaknesses are non-negotiable to the role of the employee. For instance, the head of sales cannot expect to say that he has a public speaking problem and not work on it, because the nature of his role demands him to be good at public speaking. The same applies to developers who cannot code, or testers who cannot write test cases.

Nevertheless, the idea is that employees work on their weaknesses just enough to make them serviceable, and spend all the other time working on adding more dimensions to their strengths. This is more efficient because

a) The return over investment of a person's strengths becoming stronger are much higher than that of weaknesses being worked on.

b) The person herself is more motivated to work on her strengths rather than on her weaknesses.

The aim is to manage the weaknesses and focus on the strengths rather than forget about the strengths and work overtime on weaknesses.

Alas, while this change is happening and it's heartening to see, the vast majority of organizations in India today still adhere to the old way. The employee's strengths are almost glossed over as an afterthought, and a whole lot of time and deliberation is devoted to her weaknesses as well as strategies that could be adopted to convert them into strengths.

As a manager, your first task is to have a working knowledge of all your team members' strengths and weaknesses. And then you should use that knowledge to complement their combination such that strengths of one person support the weaknesses of another. If you find a blanket weakness or two that you need to address, by all means communicate it to the team at large and organize a training workshop or mentorship activities to overcome it.

But your mantra should be to support your employee's weaknesses, and trust her strengths.

Don't Just Inform, Inspire.

Have you ever been to a project kick-off meeting where all the stakeholders are herded into a conference room and the manager holds court? Don't you think these rooms resemble war rooms, with everyone sweating in spite of the air conditioning? I've been to many such meetings, and I've always been struck by how incredibly stressed everyone becomes at these places.

The same could be said about *problem project* or *critical project* meetings, where everyone knows things are going horribly wrong but no one knows what to do to stop the rot.

In my humble opinion, as a manager, it is your responsibility to absorb stress.

I know we spoke earlier about the importance of communicating to your team members everything about the project and the desired results. However, if a client gave you a tough time in the morning's meeting because the project is not progressing as per his expectations. Is it necessary for you to call a meeting of your team and relay the message down to them? I don't think so. Everything that you think will elevate stress levels in your team, keep it to yourself. You're the leader. You're being paid to drive performance in your team, not anxiety.

Communication with your team members ought to be rational, logical, and as free from emotion as possible. What they need to know from you is the expectation of results. What you need to know from them is how they are moving toward the expectation. If they're ahead of the curve, congratulate them and encourage them to keep going. If they're behind, ask if they need any help or support from you. Everything else—the client calls, the underlying stress, the bickering—is just unnecessary noise for your team. So don't burden them with it.

Following Up Effectively

For delegation to be successful, the manager and the employee should first agree to a follow-up schedule in advance. You will do well to get the team member's agreement to it, just to ensure that expectations are set mutually from the beginning. This process of arriving at a follow-up schedule should also be done with the employee, rather than the manager laying down the law.

As ever, the art of conversation has very little to do with how much you talk and has almost everything to do with how much you listen. Asking questions and genuinely listening to your employees is a skill that you will use often. You could perhaps say something like "Do you think once a week is a good enough to begin with?" and see what your employee says in response. "Maybe starting with a fortnight before release, we could do a daily checkpoint, just so we're all on the same page. What do you think?"

Whatever follow-up schedule you decide upon, make it extremely clear to your team member that she is more than welcome to approach you in case a problem occurs. More projects go down the drain due to the employee's shyness to knock on their manager's door in a timely fashion over any other reason. As a manager, it is your responsibility to impress upon your team the necessity of flagging issues as soon as they come up.

Lastly, it is important that you put the onus on the employee to give you updates, with you interfering with their work only if and when you spot a report that does not make sense or that needs further clearing up. Stick to the spirit of delegation, and trust your employees to do their jobs well without you having to breathe fire down their necks.

In my long working career before I became an entrepreneur I have had rich experience in working for good, bad and ugly bosses!

One quality that distinguishes a good boss is their style of delegation.

I was working for an Ad firm and my last boss turned out to be a great boss.

I recall one incident where he demonstrated what effective delegation is all about.

After having worked with him closely for over 2 years, I noticed that he was giving me more and more responsibility and somewhere in my mind, I got the feeling that he was grooming me for bigger things.

A major client pitch was coming up and for the most part of the preparation for the presentation; my boss was laid up with a back problem.

As the date for the pitch was getting closer, I was getting a little nervous because he had still not recovered and was overseeing the development of the pitch from his home. The team and I kept going back and forth showing him stuff until he gave us the green signal for putting the whole thing together.

Closer toward the date of the pitch, my boss was getting better and it was understood that he and I would go together for the presentation.

The day before the presentation, we went through the presentation and the stage was set for me to lead the presentation.

On the morning of the important date, I got a call from him and, to my utter surprise, he told me that he would not be joining me for the presentation and that I was on my own!

I was shocked! I had never done this before, and given the size of the opportunity, I was certainly over awed.

He would not hear any of my pleas and wished me all the best.

The pitch went well and we won the account. Later on, in a conversation with my boss, I came to know that all along he was grooming me to replace him, and the pitch was one of the first tests for me to pass!

I recall another incident where I decided to walk out of a client and he backed me to the hilt even though the client tried to reach him to have me sacked from the account.

This is a great example of trust and empowerment and of course competency building is a given.

Bad delegation is more the rule than the exception. At every level in the organization, managers are operating at one or even two levels below their designated roles! A General Manager does the work of the Regional Manager. The project manager does the work of a Team Lead and so on.

Ideally, a true professional will strive to operate at one level higher or at least at the level at which they are designated.

Micromanaging often comes from a lack of trust in the employee coupled with a sense of insecurity.

"What if my subordinate does a better job than the manager?"

I recall a participant at one of my leadership development programs sharing the story of one such micromanager. He would be the first to come to work and the last to leave. Always stressed out, foul tempered, kicking, screaming, and pulling up people in full glare of everyone.

Every decision had to go through him, and he made sure that he always recruited people who were much less capable than he was.

When he moved out of the team, he had left behind a slow team, stunted and incapable of making even the smallest decisions.

This project team had to be disbanded since they could not be assigned independent charge of even a small project. A few folks even lost their jobs!

Conclusions

In this chapter, we looked a bit more deeply into the topic of delegation. The salient points we discussed are:

- Delegation is an instinctively difficult thing to do, with cultural, personal, and interpersonal reasons impeding us. One of the most difficult aspects of delegation is to distance oneself from one's work, which is hard to do while maintaining a keen interest in it.

- A manager should delegate results and not tasks. He should treat his team members as responsible individuals who can be trusted, not as mindless robots.
- A manager should inspire his team in addition to informing them. An effective way to do this is to act as a *stress sponge*, where he absorbs all the negative energy coming from the management above and radiates only positive energy onto his team.
- Support an individual's weaknesses, and trust his strengths. If possible, combine team members so that one person's weakness is supported by another's strengths and vice versa.
- Following up effectively is an important part of delegation. A manager should ideally agree with an employee in advance about a follow-up schedule.
- Teams should be told unequivocally that the door to the manager's cabin is always open when it comes to flagging issues that could potentially alter the project's schedule.
- Leave the onus up to the team to give you reports, and only intervene when a report appears strange or needs further clarity. Just

UNMANAGE

leave your team alone to do their work, and you do yours.

CHAPTER FIFTEEN

Empowerment

Ask any manager what she wants from her team and she's bound to throw the word empowerment into her answer. This is the new buzzword of the business world.

Empowered teams need little management. Members of an empowered team take ownership and responsibility, understand the full consequences of the solution they're working on, and are honest, upright, and loyal. They have fun at work, they help each other out, and they function as one single unit with a common goal. Conflicts don't arise, and when they do, empowered teams resolve them swiftly and with decisiveness.

In short, everything is pink and rosy.

However, managers too often make the mistake of thinking that empowerment just happens as a random act of magic rather than thinking of it as an ideal worth pursuing. In my view, empowerment is a consequence of the first fourteen chapters of this book. As a manager, if you:

- Understand your management style and natural personality
- Work on your integrity, trust and credibility
- Focus on the fine balance between results, processes and relationships
- Develop an environment of transparency, in which you delegate effectively to your team members
- Prioritize your employees' motivations and thirst for appreciation over anything else

Empowerment will automatically happen, without you needing to chase it consciously. In this chapter, I will share a case study of a project where I was privileged to see empowered team members working together. Where possible, I will try to point out any lessons or takeaways for us to employ in our own individual management styles.

CHAPTER SIXTEEN

The Human Side of Business

We live in a time of great material excess. Whatever indicator we use for wealth and physical health, the twenty-first century has seen immense advances. One would think that being alive in an age of history where material wealth is at its highest and disease is on the back foot will make us happy.

Alas! We're not any happier than we were a century ago, or even two centuries ago. Granted, it is not easy to measure intangibles such as happiness and discontent, but I don't think anyone of us would deny that it is those intangibles we live for. One of the most basic goals of human existence is **to be happy** not *to earn this much,* or *to travel to these many countries,* or *to buy so many houses.*

We only chase the material because we think that it will lead us to that intangible. Yet now we're richer. We're healthier. We live longer. But we aren't any happier. This is perhaps the fundamental paradox of our age of excess wealth. What is it that we're missing in this mad rush for more?

A warning: this chapter will deal with abstract concepts such as fulfillment and meaning, so if you're expecting mathematical equations out of which happiness springs, then you will be disappointed. Life is not a math problem. The trouble is that too often, we treat it that way.

So I will encourage you to step out of your management shoes for this chapter, and put on your human shoes. Let's not talk about revenue, deadlines, compliance, and discipline for a while.

Let's instead ponder on what makes us tick as human beings. What drives you out of your bed every morning? How do you feel on a Sunday evening, with a week of work ahead of you? In this section, we will return to the sentiment with which we started the book: in order to be a good manager, one must be a good human being. And in order to understand what motivates your team, you must understand what motivates you.

The Human Value System

One of the hardest questions I'd ever had to answer was when—after years in training and teaching the subject—I was asked by a student in one of my classes, "How do you define a value?"

My first instinct was to snub her, and chide her for being so enamored by definitions instead of embracing concepts in the abstract space. However, on a little reflection, it struck me that she was not really asking me for a definition of a value; she was asking me for direction on how to examine her value system and appraise it.

It took me only a few moments of thought to realize that my values are no different from yours or someone else's. All human beings have value systems instilled into them by society and nature. If I could be allowed to write them down, here is a basic list:

1. **Loyalty.** We're all traders, and wired deep into our DNA is the concept of *you scratch my back, and I will scratch yours. If I scratch your back today, I expect you to do the same tomorrow.* This expectation of loyalty extends into our social lives as well, where a friend's gift to you on your birthday puts you under pressure to buy her an equally good gift when she celebrates hers. This sense of giving back what you get seems to be a quality that exists within animals too, so perhaps this is not so much a learned behavior as it is a natural one.
2. **Justice.** Close on the heels of loyalty comes this idea of justice, an expectation that good deeds will be rewarded and bad deeds will be punished. We expect to be treated justly by others and we treat them justly in return.
3. **Love.** Maybe the most powerful value that drives social human life on the planet. This could be further divided broadly into filial love—the love you feel for your kith and kin, and romantic love—the love you feel for your unrelated partners through life.
4. **Forgiveness.** This is not so much a natural behavior as it is learned. Some of us forgive more easily than others, and it flies in the face

of our expectations of justice and loyalty. After all, much of forgiveness becomes necessary when we're treated unjustly or when someone breaks our trust.

This is by no means a definitive list. Traits such as honesty, trust, kindness, and humility could easily appear on similar lists compiled by other people. I'm sure your list will be different from mine. Nevertheless, once I made my list, it occurred to me that almost everyone around me has, essentially, the same list. And yet we're different as people. What causes this difference?

I can't help but think that even though your values are virtually the same as mine when they're listed out, you become different to me in two respects:

1. In your relative preference of one value over another. For instance, you may hold forgiveness dearer to your heart than you hold love, so you may forgive betrayal more easily than I do.
2. The amount of laxity you allow yourself. In other words, how big a temptation does it take to make you break your values and turn the other way? For instance, I may hold the value of being ethical dear to my heart, but a temptation could potentially sway me from being true to the value. The necessary size of the temptation could be different for you and

me. You may never sway no matter what the bargain.

What is true of people is also true of corporations. We all define ourselves by those values that we hold dear and follow no matter what. When I look at my own situation, I like to make the demarcation between core values and fluid values. Core values are those that I will never make a compromise on, no matter how big the carrot dangling at the end of the stick is. Fluid values are those that I believe in and admire, and I do follow them when it is convenient for me to do so, but there exists a temptation large enough to sway me away from them. I will be guilt-ridden for a while after that, of course, but I will make my peace with it.

Whether we like to admit it or not, we all have these two concentric circles in our heads: one rigid, cold, rock-hard, unchanging, and the other, outer one made of plasma, where values and choices intermingle freely depending on situations.

What will help in your own journey as a manager is the knowledge of your own value system. Let no one cast judgment on how good or bad your core and fluid values are. If at the end of this thought experiment you realize that you're not willing to compromise on any of your values, so be it. If, on the other hand, you realize that everything in your value system is negotiable, that is also fine. This is not a question of what is good or bad, but what kind of person you are, and what kind of manager you're likely to be.

I will end this section with a small note. Keep in mind that this balance between fluid and core values itself is constantly changing. In your teens, you may have more core values than fluid, and by the time you enter the workplace, the balance may have shifted a little. By the time you hit your forties, with a marriage, kids and a mid-life crisis to juggle, some more values may swim from the hard inner circle to the vacuous outer circle (or in the reverse direction).

A Company's Values

It is a cliché, but only because it is true. A company is nothing more than the sum total of people working for it. So a corporation is a living, breathing entity just like a human being, and like human beings, it should have a value system that it holds dear. Often an organization's management practice is derived from its values—core and flexible.

Not to belabor the point but many of today's companies—even those that are supposed to be great—are run with only one thing in mind: the balance sheet. Some businesses are revenue-focused (top line focus) and some are profit-focused (bottom line), but you hardly see any CEO anymore talking about the values that his company stands for and is trying to protect.

Earlier it used to be that values and good practice led to profits and revenue as a holistic consequence. Now managers start with revenue targets and work backwards to achieve them by whatever means possible.

The Sundaram Finance Story

When it comes to thinking of a stellar example of a company that believes and lives by the human side of business, the Chennai headquartered Sundaram Finance (SF), an NBFC, tops my list. Here is a company that's been around for sixty-five years now in one of the most challenging and fiercely competitive industries—retail financing.

Founded by Shri T S Santhanam in 1954, the founder chairman laid the foundations of a unique culture built around a set of values that the company has lived by all these years. These are Sundaram Finance's stated values that every employee intuitively practices not because the organization has mandated it but because they resonate with them.

As words, they may seem simplistic but every single value has defined the company in the minds and hearts of its stakeholders.

The values are Service, Fair play, Prudence, Relationships, Integrity, Honesty, Discipline, Openness and Humility.

While most organizations benchmark themselves with metrics like profitability, growth rate, market share, head count, etc. SF chose a different path. They chose the path of customer experience, employee concern, depositor peace of mind, compliance, and transparency. They have evolved through the decades dedicated to performance in the present with **a commitment to sustainability in the long term.**

It is true that SF is not the fastest growing NBFC. SF is not the highest paymaster when it comes to employee compensation. Their profits are not the highest, and most surprisingly, their lending rates are not the lowest! And yet, customers, employees, and depositors all gravitate toward SF and insist that they would never willingly want to dissociate from the company.

How to explain this strange phenomenon? It has to do with their firm belief that at the end of the day, the people matter over all else! And when people matter most, values become the compass. It isn't a wonder that anyone who comes in contact with SF talks about the *Sundaram experience*, and this cannot be explained by breaking it down to a model or a framework, simply because it defies definition and transcends corporate logic. There appears to be an all-pervasive *Corporate Conscience* that every employee intuitively taps into while making decisions and taking action. It cannot be broken down into a case study and copied by other companies.

And that's because it has got to be lived! Every single employee lives it every day in the farthest parts of their pan India presence.

Through a unique model of *Gurukula*, a combination of word-of-mouth informal mentoring, peer counseling, and transparent thinking, Sundaram Finance has been able to inspire generations of employees into becoming the ambassadors of a values based culture of service as the foundation of lasting relationships.

The secret sauce is that there is no secret sauce, just a simple steadfast commitment to a set of timeless values in the increasingly confusing world we live in.

Case Study: Orangescape Technologies Limited

Background

OrangeScape is a leading cloud-based B2B software company offering KiSSFLOW—a disruptive SaaS platform for collaborative work management. OrangeScape's KiSSFLOW was conceived with the belief that simple things should stay simple and complex things should be possible, with the mission to reduce chaos in every office. Top industry analysts Gartner & Forrester have featured KiSSFLOW making it a disrupter in its category. KiSSFLOW has a global footprint with users across 160 countries, including many Fortune 500 companies such as Airbus, Motorola, and Reckitt Benckiser.

> "Happy Employees make Happy Customers. Our approach to creating Happy Customers is deeply rooted in nurturing an organizational environment where our employees enjoy doing great work working together."
>
> Suresh Sambandam (CEO, OrangeScape)

Path Breaking People Practices at OrangeScape

The CEO's statement gives a clear rationale. It explains the "why" (the core of the golden circle re: Simon Sinek) behind OrangeScape's approach to its people. They do not merely imitate popular practices or run multiple initiatives but check to see how any proposed practice aligns with their core beliefs. This also means that they choose to work or invest in practices that will help build and strengthen the culture they wish to permeate through their organization for a long time.

1. Hiring

Hiring is often the most underrated lever to build a great organization despite enough being spoken about it. At a very simple level, it is junk in junk out. Hence hiring has been identified as a key lever to shape culture. OrangeScape is front-loading their people investment i.e. spending more time and money in getting the hiring process right, to get the right people into the right role. The process is constantly evaluated to ensure that every new candidate increases the overall average of the team.

   a. The final interview for all positions is conducted by the CEO to check 'values alignment' with the six core values namely: All for One, Bias to Action, Be Learning, Craft

Memorable Experiences, Speak Up, 20/20 Vision. The CEO takes a call on every individual who joins by spending one-on-one time before any hiring decision is made.

b. The sales team designs and executes its own interviewing process to ensure better fitment of hired candidates. When the scale of hiring increased, the quality was maintained by ensuring the business team was hands-on during the entire process. They were able to directly handpick candidates as well as and establish a relationship from an early stage.

c. Unorthodox yet genuine approaches have been rewarded with an interview. The company has interviewed and hired people who have directly reached out to the CEO over social media.

2. Operating as Squads

One of the key issues with scaling is the tendency for teams to become bloated and lose the drive and connect of a small unit. As a result, performance levels invariably plateau. The structuring of teams into squads enabled the organization to grow big without losing the agility and speed of a small unit. Squads are made up of individuals from different functional teams coming together to work on a specific project. This means squads are goal-oriented and possess heterogeneous skill sets. The typical squad size is no bigger than a team that can be fed by two pizzas!

3. Working in Public: Shift from Emails to Internal Social Media

Collaboration and transparency are ideas that have been espoused by most companies but few really introspect on their daily practices to see if they truly live up to or hinder these values. Let's take emails as the default mode of professional communication. They have been accepted as a necessary evil of professional life. But emails also create boundaries around people and projects with no visibility. And this goes against OrangeScape's stated goal of having a transparent work culture.

Honestly, OrangeScape did not have this clarity in the beginning, but as they gave more thought to the tension between their aspirational and practical culture, they knew practical steps had to be taken. They decided to remove emails as their default or primary mode of communication within the organization. This is a paradigm shift in working. They embraced a culture of "Working in Public." This can be scary because it requires tremendous self-confidence to share ideas publicly and overcome apprehensions of being perceived as perceptions of showing off. But the payoffs are immense. They have not only increased speed of decision-making but also have federated knowledge (knowledge locked in with small groups that are now open to all who are interested). By making all work groups open, anyone can see what any team is working on. However, individuals have to be interested (pull not push). The onus is on them. This is real transparency and collaboration. It was done quickly and seamlessly. Now, it is a way of life.

They realized that it was a lack of imagination and trust rather than practical issues that prevent most companies from embracing this philosophy of extreme trust.

4. G2G (Good to Great)
G2G is a program at OrangeScape where the entire organization comes together (physically) for one hour every week to learn from and with each other. While the content varies, the objective has remained constant—learning + bonding + fun. This is non-negotiable as it ensures that company DNA is transmitted and the relationships strengthened as they scale. Past activities include book reading (Good to Great, Delivering Happiness), employee interest groups (teaching by employees to employees), core values creation and evangelization, team building workshops etc.

5. OrangeScape Leadership Program (OLP)
Succession planning and building leaders at every level of the organization are critical if one has to realize the gains of growth. OrangeScape has handpicked a group of young leads and managers to

go on a one-year leadership journey along with the senior leadership of the organization. The group is intentionally large (compared to the organization's size) and diverse (across all departments) to give everyone in a managerial capacity the best chance to be successful. The consistent connect over time helps people test, dialogue, and internalize the learnings. Participants and the senior leadership (including the CEO) commit one Saturday every month to this learning journey. The programs are conducted outside the office to allow people to immerse themselves in the learning.

6. Writers' Workshop

With a vision to build thought leaders in the organization, they invested in two editions of a writing workshop. They made this conscious and maybe even unorthodox investment as an organization because they want to build clarity and articulation skills among their people. Each workshop had around eighteen employees (across all departments) who were largely non-writers. They were taken through a two-day workshop to help them get started on the journey of being thought leaders. This was followed by a 100-day challenge where each participant set himself or herself an ambitious writing target (the highest was 100 blogs by an employee in 100 days).

This was made possible by the group agreeing to meet together and write for 15–30 minutes every day at lunch. It served to keep the motivation strong for 100 days. The challenge ended with an organization wide celebration with Rashmi Bansal as the chief guest.

What started as a simple idea to generate content for their "Behind the Peel" company blog has blossomed into something memorable. They also realized that this is the best way to share their culture. When someone sees people writing poems and stories of individual development on the official platform, any reader from outside can directly infer about the company culture. They are happy to have hit on a formula that develops their employees and showcases the company!

7. Co-creating Core Values
The quest is to articulate culture. They wanted something that would remain non-negotiable, relevant across all departments, simple, and, most importantly, meaningful to everyone. This meant that they had to discover and define what they stood for—their core values. They ensured that this would not be a top down exercise or a hurried activity. They created a set of questions that the entire organization would respond to and culled out their core values from it. The final list was then openly and feverishly debated upon before everyone went in for a vote. With this, they came up with their six core values with a simple acronym "ABB-CSV."

I. All for One - We are one team with one goal. Support, celebrate, and trust each other.
II. Bias to action - Experiment, fail, learn, share, repeat. Seek forgiveness instead of permission.
III. Be Learning - Seek out new experiences, question the obvious, and start your journey to mastery.
IV. Craft Memorable Experiences - Leave a lasting, world-class impression on the minds of customers and colleagues.
V. Speak Instead - Debate issues, not people. Handle conflicts directly with trust and respect.
VI. 20/20 Vision - Your work matters. Have total clarity on how what you do helps us reach our goals.

The organization's idea was for them to be a part of their people and not just a poster on the wall or a website. Thus, they embarked on a six-month journey to evangelize the core values. The employees themselves took ownership of how this would be done. It resulted in regular and wider discussion of the core values with each person constantly clarifying their understanding of what it means, and why it is important and most importantly how it impacts their daily work.

8. Voice of Employees

Though it is still a small enough organization for employees to connect directly, they realize that different people tend to voice their opinions differently. They have designed multiple mechanisms to ensure that they hear everyone. Rather than run generic surveys, the People Ops team and the CEO co-designed the annual engagement surveys. The results and analysis are shared back with the teams to put them in practice. In addition to this, they have a half-yearly organizational offsite where organization and department updates are shared. They also have AMA (Ask Me Anything) where questions can be raised anonymously and responses are documented online for all to discuss and track. There are also one-on-one discussions with the CEO.

9. CTO Talk

Any work on the company's culture exercise is not complete without contributing to the ecosystem. They believe culture cannot be shaped or sustained without giving back to society. They saw that there were many events happening in Chennai but not enough at the highest levels of technology innovation with brands that solve problems for a billion people and more. They felt this learning would benefit the entire tech ecosystem in terms of idea generation and job creation. Thus, began CTO Talk by OrangeScape.

CTO Talk is India's first knowledge sharing platform exclusively by and for CTOs. It is a monthly series where they provide a rare, deep learning opportunity for aspiring tech leaders and have CTOs from well-known brands such as Flipkart, Snapdeal, Naukri, and Swiggy come in as guest speakers. CTOs dive into how they built scalability into their businesses.

10. Career Shifts / Readjustments

In a fast growing start up, roles and responsibilities are typically redefined with new opportunities opening up. Looking outside for talent is an option but a wrong hire (skill set or culture mismatch) can stick out like a sore thumb in a small team. Therefore, the other option that they devised is to identify internal talent from different roles and reposition them, so that they can deliver more value while continuing to be part of the team. Sometimes this means identifying latent skills that might help them flourish in a completely different field that even they might not have thought of. The organization helps them to make the transition through intensive training, hands on mentoring, and regular feedback to maximize their chances of success.

11. Gender Diversity

When it began, its employees joked that OrangeScape resembled a boys' hostel. Today, 35 percent of the organization is made up of women. Providing them with a safe and comfortable working environment is a priority. This rapid and significant shift was made possible only because everyone in the company played an active role in ensuring that the workplace was welcoming to talented people of either gender.

Afterword

In writing this book, my prism has been the Indian corporate world and Indian managers.

I have had a ringside view of the growth of the Indian economy and Indian companies over the last 2 decades.

I am seeing all the signs of capitalism with its pros and cons, taking over the Indian economy and materialism gripping every Indian. Over a billion people have cell phones and the poorest home sprouts a dish antenna.

Like the West, I am seeing a steady erosion of values being traded for profits and unprecedented levels of corruption largely because of the politician-business nexus.

This pursuit of greed and growth for growth's sake is taking a toll at every level of human relationships—

boss-employee, peer-to-peer, spouses, parent-child—and that is cause for concern.

Considering that work occupies 80 percent of our waking lives, I think companies and leaders in organizations must show the way forward by reinforcing values in everyday life.

This is where I believe that each of us can make a difference. Can we be the sane voice that speaks up when we see blatant abuse of power at work or at home?

Or in our social lives?

Can we hold people accountable for their actions?

When we build people the right way, we build families, organizations and societies that value human relationships over all else.

We have been managing for all the wrong reasons. Now let us UNMANAGE for all the right reasons.

APPENDIX I

Company Case Studies

Rise and Fall of HMT

In 2014, the Indian government decided to wind up HMT, the pioneer watch manufacturer in India. This company dominated the watch market in India from the 1960s to mid-1990. In the years that followed, HMT lost its market share to its single largest competitor Titan. This however did not happen overnight.

HMT had the unique privilege of being asked to set up a watch manufacturing facility by the government of India in 1961. HMT was selected because it had quite a reputation for manufacture of high precision tools. The company had the early mover advantage and went from strength to strength. It set up manufacturing facilities in Bangalore, Srinagar, Tumkur, and Kumaon. Ancillary units were also set up to provide employment to small scale industries. The product portfolio of HMT consisted of Mechanical watches.

In the 1960s, a group of businessmen from the French watch making town, Besancon, joined an Indian collaborator to form the Indo-French Time Industries Pvt. Ltd. in Mumbai. They imported high quality French parts and sold watches named Timestar. This was the only serious competition that HMT faced at that time. According to estimates, the number of imported Swiss watches fell from around a million in 1955 to just twelve thousand in 1980. This drove the retailers to stock HMT watches. HMT benefitted from the government policy of clamping down on imports of watches.

Up to this time (1981), sales of HMT watches were really high. Even though the demand for HMT watches was high, retailers were not happy stocking HMT watches because they felt that the French brands like Favre-Leuba were doing well. HMT then started sales of watches through its thirteen offices. Until then, these offices sold machine tools.

The company invested in a lot of market research to study buyer behavior, demand patterns, and the like. This prompted the company to diversify into manufacture of quartz watches. Quartz watches affected the business of traditional Swiss watchmakers. However, HMT could not capitalize on this because the quartz watches were very chunky and battery replacements were not available freely and were also expensive.

HMT then stepped back to mechanical watches and dumped quartz manufacture. The government aided by not allowing import of quartz components. At this time, the world had switched to quartz watches.

Thanks to the economic liberalization in the mid-1980s, import restrictions were lifted and prices of quartz fell. HMT faced stiff competition from the new entrant Titan (joint venture of Tata's and TIDCO)

Titan made a quartz—only entry into the Indian market. They set up a two million watch manufacturing facility in Hosur, Tamilnadu. The entry of Titan watches accompanied heavy advertising support. The company came in with around eight hundred and fifty models. The product team was manned by graphic designers. Titan also decided to bypass the wholesale channel. It set up standalone retail outlets and consumer experience was the focus. Mood windows were set up to enhance the buying experience. The company also forayed into jewelry and jewelry watches in 1994. These products were branded as Tanishq, and they entered the domestic market and later the European market.

In response to this surge in demand for quartz watches, HMT set up a design center for the first time in 1991. In 1994, Titan made a profit of nineteen crores and HMT made a loss of sixty crores. HMT watches began to die.

Despite restructuring itself into different groups, the momentum was lost. HMT attempted to sell assembled watches, but this model also suffered. HMT did not keep with the times.

In October 2014, the government decided to close down sick units and took a decision to close down HMT.

TVS Group – Success with Liberalization

TVS was established by T. V. Sundaram Iyengar. Born in 1877, he began with Madurai's first bus service in 1911 and founded T.V.Sundaram Iyengar and Sons Ltd., a company that consolidated its presence in the transportation business with a large fleet of trucks and buses under the name of Southern Roadways Ltd.

When he died in 1955, his sons took the company ahead with several forays in the automobile sector including finance, insurance, manufacture of two wheelers, tires, and its components. The group has managed to run thirty-three companies with a combined turnover of nearly five billion dollars.

Some of the prominent companies in the TVS group are Sundaram Fasteners, Lucas TVS, Brakes India, Wheels India, Sundaram Brake Linings, TVS Motor Company, and TVS Electronics. These companies with their ability to deliver products of the right quality, at the right price and at the right time have made a mark in the Indian and global markets. Underlying the success of the group is its philosophy of trust, value, and service.

Sundaram Clayton was the earliest flagship company. Founded in collaboration with Clayton Dewandre Holdings, UK, it manufactured brakes, exhausts, compressors, and various other automotive parts. A plant was set up in Hosur in 1978 to manufacture mopeds as part of a new division.

In 1982, the company tied up with Suzuki Motor Corporation. The joint venture corporation was called Ind-Suzuki Ltd.

1980 is an important milestone in the Indian two wheeler industry. TVS 50, India's first moped was launched. This ushered an era of affordable personal transportation.

This was a period of very challenging economic climate in India. The cost of manufacturing was very high. It was a tight license regime.

However, post 1991, companies were able to raise money and manufacturers became competitive. India became an attractive destination for MNCs. Banking opened up and exports grew. Capital convertibility was introduced. This helped India Inc. to establish itself overseas.

TVS and Suzuki shared a nineteen-year long relationship that was aimed at technology transfer to enable design and manufacture of two wheelers specifically for the Indian market. A number of models such as Suzuki Samurai, Suzuki Shogun, and Suzuki Fiero were released under the joint venture. However, differences in opinion as to how to run the joint venture eventually led to the partners moving different ways. Even before it broke off its association with Suzuki, the company had, on its own steam developed a number of successful mopeds and scooters. The model *Victor* was a huge hit and sold more than sixty thousand vehicles since 2001.

After the split in 2001, the company has now been renamed TVS Motor. It relinquished its right to use the Suzuki name. There was a thirty-month moratorium period when Suzuki promised not to enter the Indian market. There was a lot of labor unrest and Chairman Venu Srinivasan had to take tough measures to resurrect the company. He invested in new technology, nurtured in-house design, and implemented quality programs.

TVS motor backed up its efforts in design and engineering by major investments in plant and machinery to produce their new products in large volumes with the latest manufacturing techniques. The company outsourced technologies and designs for sub-assemblies but managed the integrity of the design of the product.

The company, over the years has grown to be the largest in the group, both in terms of size and turnover with four state of the art manufacturing companies—three in India and one in Indonesia.

In July 2012, TVS motors tied up with BMW Motorrad to aim to develop and produce motorcycles in the sub500cc category.

In July 2013, the company planned to construct a motorcycle assembling plant in Uganda. The idea was to introduce new models suitable for the East African market. They had commissioned a plant earlier in Kenya too.

In conclusion, we can well say that liberalization allowed the TVS group to use its technological capability, fill gaps through imports, and integrate these abilities with understanding of the market to launch successful products. Liberalization allowed the family business group to use their entrepreneurial instincts to grow and build their businesses.

TVS believes that the success of any enterprise is built on the solid foundation of customer satisfaction. Continuous innovation and close customer interaction has enabled them to stay ahead of competition. Quality at TVS determines not only the end product but the systems, processes and operations at all levels.

The various awards that some of the group companies have won stand testimony to this.

Awards
Most of the group companies have received prestigious awards through the years.

Sundaram Fasteners, which manufactures fasteners, radiator caps, powder metal parts, cold extruded parts, hot forged parts, pumps and assemblies was the first Indian company to have the ISO certification. They also have been awarded the *Supplier of the Year* award by General Motors for five consecutive years. This is the first Indian company to have this credit.

TVS Motor Company Ltd. is the first two wheeler company in the world to have been awarded the Deming prize in 2002. This is the most coveted award for total quality management.

Brakes India, a group company has also been awarded the Deming prize in 2003.

Commitment to its people is a fundamental principle of the TVS management philosophy. The group's concern for the development and welfare of its employees is deep rooted. From providing drinking water to villages to setting up schools and hospitals, TVS contributes actively to the development of local communities.

Taj Hotels Case Story

The Taj Mahal Hotel project was based on an incident where Jamshetji Nusserwanji Tata was denied entry into a city hotel for being an Indian. This incident left such a deep scar in his psyche, and he decided to construct a place equally luxurious and lavish for all fellow Indians. He decided to build the Taj Mahal Hotel in Bombay in 1893 on land leased from the Bombay Port trust for ninety-nine years. His sisters were the first to object to his idea of opening a *bhatarkhana* (eating house). But Jamshetji went ahead with his plan and opened its doors on December 16, 1903. Going by the advice of their astrologer, the 10,000 sq. ft. hotel opened with its central dome incomplete and only one floor ready. Electricity was a problem and lifts were not in working condition too. The hotel did not do well. Jamshetji wanted to sell it, but he couldn't, for the only reason that the kitchen was in the top floor. Jamshetji had no choice but to complete the construction of the hotel, because he had already spent twenty lakhs on it, which was a very big sum in those times.

Jamshetji died in Germany in 1904. His successor had great trouble too with the hotel. However, in order to salvage some finances, parts of the hotel were rented out as petrol distribution centers, sales rooms for motor cars and garage for taxi service.

The Indian princes loved the hotel as it offered them many informal privileges like drinking beer. Since they loved the hotel, one of them very generously offered a debenture loan of two lakhs. At that time, the hotel was considering offers from Ritz, J.Lyons etc.

When JRD Tata took over the hotel, he too felt that the hotel had to be sold as it was run badly. In November 1933, India had its first AC restaurant-cum-ballroom, and its most famous bar inside Taj— the Harbor Bar.

Business picked up well but the government passed the prohibition law and again the hotel slipped into the red, and the management seriously considered its closure. However, the war saved the day when army men began using the hotel. Prohibition was partially lifted in 1940 and the hotel made an all-time profit of five lakhs, equaling the all-time high it reached in 1918.

Taj's post-war decline started by the summer of 1947. In 1962, Colonel Leslie Sawhney took over. He was Dorabji Tata's brother-in-law. He hired a professional hotelier in London by name Ajit Kerkar. He was one of his trusted lieutenants. He put together a team and this young team went about making drastic changes to the interiors of the hotel, sometimes even without the approval of the board.

The hotel was then occupied all the time. The turnover in 1969–70 jumped to two point four crores compared to the four lakh in 1941. To fund its expansion plans, Indian Hotels went public.

Until the 1970s the Taj Mahal hotel was the only property of the Taj group.

With the completion of its initial public offering in early 1970s, the company expanded with properties all over India in important tourist destinations. This helped the company become a leading hotel chain in India. The Taj group has been active in converting former royal palaces into world class luxury hotels. The Taj Lake Palace in Udaipur, the Rambagh palace in Jaipur, and Umaid Bhavan Palace in Jodhpur are some such instances. The Taj group also opened the first five star beach resort, The Fort Aguada Beach Resort, Goa. It also began its business in Metropolitan hotels in the 1970s, opening the five star deluxe hotel Taj Coromandel in 1974. The Taj President opened in 1977 in Mumbai and the

Taj Mahal hotel opened in Delhi in 1978. In 1980, The Taj group crossed the Indian shores and set up a hotel in Sanaa in Yemen. Then came the Crown Plaza, James Court London, in the late 1980s. This was followed by 51 Buckingham luxury suites and apartments in London. In 1984, the group made its foray into Bangalore, followed by Taj Bengal in Kolkata in 1989. With this, the group had a presence in all five major cities in India.

For years, the Indian domestic hotel sector had grown in isolation, with a handful of hospitality chains—the Taj, Oberoi, Leela, Ashok, Ambassador among them—laying claim to the organized market. When the doors of this market swung wide open, India became a favored destination for as many as forty-seven international brands.

Intense competition in the market place led to what the CEO Mr. Bicksen calls *a two-pronged strategy*. The company's most significant move was to create a new brand architecture, where the single Taj brand was supplemented by new brands. In 2008, the company started carving up its hotel portfolio into four unique and distinct sub brands that have clearly differentiated brand propositions across all price segments of the market.

At the very top is the Taj Hotels Resorts and Palaces brand, a luxury offering covering ultra-premium hospitality experiences, ranging from heritage palaces to exotic safaris. The premium of upper-upscale brand Vivanta straddles the four and five star categories. Three star business travelers looking for quality comfort is the target of the Gateway brand and the Ginger chain of hotels occupies the budget sector.

Hospitality is a people business and the Taj's standard of service is very high. "Taj had to stand out as the luxury brand," explains Deepa Misra Harris, senior vice president (sales and marketing). "Vivanta by Taj is an offering in the premium segment and that's why the name is an extension of the Taj brand. Gateway and Ginger are not luxury brands and they do not need the Taj endorsement; they have the strength to stand alone."

The new architecture enabled IHCL to be more nimble and to maintain its market leadership position with each sub-brand mapping its growth plan. "We intend to remain the dominant player in the domestic market, and to build up our international presence significantly," says Abhijit Mukherjee, Executive Director, Hotel Operations.

The expansion spree is being orchestrated with a high degree of caution, though. IHCL has burned fingers with high value properties and is now consciously following a policy of asset-light growth. Instead of outright purchases, it is increasingly looking at leased properties, joint ventures and management contracts, domestically as well as internationally. Six of the company's seven new properties slated to open in India this year will be operated through management contracts instead of the traditional ownership or investment model.

IHCL is using the alliances and partnerships route to grow its brand visibility. It has tied up with American Express in a loyalty program. Similar loyalty tie-ups are in place with twenty airlines and one of the world's leading cruise lines, Silversea Cruises. The company is also collaborating with other hotel chains in regions where it does not have a presence, such as the Okura Hotel in Japan and the Victoria Jungfrau in Switzerland. Besides, IHCL has beefed up its own loyalty program, the Taj Inner Circle, which pulls in 12 percent of the company's revenues.

One of the key marketing pillars has been the creation of high grade, clearly differentiated guest experiences. "The Taj's biggest trump cards have been its suite of heritage palaces such as the Taj Lake Palace in Udaipur, Umaid Bhawan in Jodhpur, Rambagh Palace in Jaipur, and Falaknuma in Hyderabad, which offer guests a genuine maharaja-styled stay," says Jyoti Narang, Chief Operating Officer, India operations, Taj Luxury Hotels and Taj Safaris. "The group is fortunate to have 14 authentic palaces, ranging from small to grand, which add immensely to the mystique and aura of the Taj brand."

IHCL is now focusing on other customized hospitality offerings. "We're looking at creating similar unique experiences around the smaller palaces and some of the forts," says Ms. Harris. It has already launched its luxury nature and wildlife experiences under the Taj Safari brand. Another new offering is the Jiva Spa, a unique-to-Taj experience that attracts guests in search of wellness holidays.

Hospitality is a people business and the Taj's standard of service is so high that it has become the subject of several management case studies. As Mr. Bickson explains, "Technology can be used to improve efficiency and service, but in the end, it's the personal touch that matters—the relationship that our front-line staff forges with our guests—be it first-timers who walk into the portals of the Taj or our longstanding customers. It is this genuinely positive attitude toward service that stays on with our guests. It brings them back to the Taj, their home, time after time."

A Taj internal study shows that on an average, a guest interacts with a member of the staff forty-one times a day, starting with the wake-up call in the morning to the housekeeping, the front office, room service, and restaurant staff to the doorman in the lobby. "All these touch points and moments define your brand to that customer," says Mr. Bickson. "This is the focus of what we are all about. Each brand, in its own way, has to deliver that consistent service and message to the guest." The company intensively tracks guest satisfaction scores and conducts external audits through mystery guests to ensure that these standards are not diluted.

Needless to say, people training and engagement activities are a big investment for IHCL. Mr. Mukherjee says that the organization has one of the best reputations in the market from the human resources perspective. He says, "The industry typically has high attrition rates (about 30 percent) but at IHCL it's 18 percent. We have been voted *Best Workplace* by a Gallup study for four consecutive years. We extend several initiatives and programs to ensure that our people are looked after."

IHCL's increasing footprint has led to a healthy top line. For the past five years, the company has been focusing on improving its bottom line through energy efficiency initiatives. Mr. Mukherjee explains that the drive is *not about cost cutting but reducing wastage.*

Across the chain, hotels are bringing down energy bills by turning off the lights in empty rooms and generally being conscious of the need to minimize power consumption. High value consumables such as imported food items, butter, and cheese are being scrutinized for wastage. "We have to tread a fine line to eliminate wastage without degrading the quality of our service and guest deliverables," says Mr.

Mukherjee. "We talk to our staff and listen to their suggestions because they know best."

The company has also adopted internal programs that drive business excellence, community development, environment conservation, employee safety and health, etc. Luxury with a purpose is now a central theme for IHCL, which explains why the Taj brand, has been working to preserve many of India's heritage structures. The company also champions the cause of arts and artisans in each of its locations to create a sustainable platform for inclusive development.

IHCL has set its targets clearly. In the near term, the company having crossed the one billion dollar mark in revenues in 2007 wants to touch two billion dollar by 2017 with twenty-five thousand rooms and twenty-five destinations. To do this it will have to become more agile and nimble, and be able to adapt quickly to changes in a volatile market.

"When the market turns positive, we have to be able to quickly make up for those lost revenues by looking at other ways of making our offering attractive to the guest," says Mr. Bickson. "Ultimately it is the loyalty of our guests that will provide value to our brand, thus driving us into the next century." Therein lies the secret of an enduring brand—the single-minded focus on delivering quality service to the customer.

1. Culture of Customer service
2. Well trained workforce
3. TATA Values
4. Rooted in the tradition of Indian Hospitality
5. Professional Management

ITDC Case Study

India got its independence in 1947. At that time, the hotel industry in India was not developed at all. There were some hotels developed by British and Indian entrepreneurs, with only a few Indians owning hotels like the Taj group (Indian Hotel Company), owned by JRD Tata and the Faletti's Hotel owned by the Oberoi Group.

The important hotels built during the British period were

- The Rugby, Matheran (1876)
- The Taj Mahal Hotel, Mumbai (1900)
- The Grand, Calcutta 1930)
- The Cecil Hotels, Shimla and Muree (1935)
- The Savoy, Mussoorie (1936)

Pandit Jawaharlal Nehru addressed the UNESCO conference in Paris in 1955 and invited UNESCO to India for its next conference, an invitation promptly accepted by the organization. When his advisors reminded Nehru about the lack of facilities in New

Delhi, he decided to build a hotel and a convention centre. It was then that Hotel Ashok's construction began, while Vigyan Bhawan became Asia's first convention center. The construction of both these huge structures, though a mammoth task involving attention paid to tiniest of details, was accomplished in just fifteen months!

Pandit Nehru used to personally supervise the construction of the hotel. It is reported that he could be spotted at the construction site a number of times. The hotel initially had only three floors. The huge edifice that we see today is after two big additions, one in the 1960s when the annex and the pillarless convention hall were constructed and the other in the 1980s when the tower block came up. One of the major highlights of the hotel was its thematic rooms including the Naga suite, the Neelam suite, the Kashmir suite, Mughal suite, and the Assam suite. Interestingly, Ashok was the only hotel then to have a Cultural Advisor who helped organize entertainment events in the hotel under the concept of Ashok Theatre.

This was the first ever government investment in the hotel—the building of the Ashoka Hotel in New Delhi.

The India Tourism Development Corporation (ITDC) was set up in 1966 as a corporation under the Indian Companies Act of 1956, with the merger of Janpath Hotel India Ltd. and India Tourism Transport

Undertaking Ltd. Today, ITDC provides a complete range of tourism services including accommodation, catering, entertainment, shopping, hotel consultancy, duty free shops, and an in-house travel agency.

The government gave the tourism industry another boost when it created the Ministry of Tourism and Civil Aviation in 1967, separating it from the Ministry of Transport and Shipping, thereby recognizing that tourism was not simply about transporting people from point A to point B but had a much wider role to play in the nation's economy.

In 1975, ITDC launched its hotel business with the acquisition of a hotel in Chennai, which was rechristened Hotel Chola. The objective of ITDC's entry into the hotel industry was rooted in the concept of creating value for the nation. ITDC chose the hotel industry because of its potential to earn high levels of foreign exchange, create a tourism infrastructure, and generate large-scale direct and indirect employment.

Three Welcome Group Hotels were commissioned between 1975 and 1977; these were non-franchised hotels, inspired by the slogan "Be Indian, Buy Indian" and using Indian expertise. Ultimately, however, these hotels adopted the Sheraton system in 1978 and used the services of expatriates for the purposes of upgrading staff training and installing Sheraton operating systems all without a management contract. This gave the Welcome Group a good start. It must be noted, that it took time for these hotels to achieve substantial foreign occupancies. The tacit discouragement of foreign franchising by the government led the leading Indian hotel companies namely The Taj, the Oberoi hotels, and the Welcome Group to launch their own franchising and management programs, giving rise to indigenous franchise operations. Their focus, however, was the 5 star and 5 star deluxe categories of hotels. Such hotels were located in the prominent metropolitan cities and a few select resorts, leading to a concentration of franchised hotels in these areas. Motivated by the success stories of the hotels in the metro cities, individual entrepreneurs began constructing hotels in secondary cities/resorts during the late 1970s.

The First Tourism Policy (1982)
The first significant policy initiatives were forged in the early 1980s. With the prospect of hosting the Asian Games of 1982, the Indian Government had to start thinking about accommodating, transporting and entertaining the large number of visitors attracted by the event. This awakened a serious public interest in tourism, which was enhanced by the fact that tourism was India's largest net earner of foreign currency. The public interest was translated into the Tourism Policy of 1982, which provided an action plan based on the development of tourism circuits.

In 1996, Government of India's shareholding in ITDC was reduced to 89.97 percent. Over the years, ITDC has built a portfolio of thirty-three hotels including seven hotels as Joint Ventures with State Governments or their agencies.

ITDC suffered heavy losses from 1999–2001. The Hotel Division of ITDC made a cumulative loss of hundred and five crores. In some of the hotels, the loss exceeded sales.

The miserable performance of ITDC was as a result of:

- **Heavy employee cost** - Employee cost in ITDC was significantly higher than its competitors. Government scales of pay increased the salaries of the employees.
- **Lack of leadership at the top** - ITDC continued to work without a full time Chairman and Managing Director for many years. The parent ministry i.e. Ministry of Tourism, Government of India did not take any decision about appointment of a suitable person in this crisis-ridden phase. As a result, bureaucrats went on holding additional charges causing enormous delay in taking any business decision.
- Talk of **disinvestment** was there in the air for a decade. This was a great demotivating factor for the employees who were working in

the ITDC. There was lots of despondency, which led to lack of proper upkeep and maintenance of the hotel leading to a bad name for the entire organization. It had a spiraling effect in the form of little occupancy in the hotels. The hospitality industry was also on the down turn and ITDC hotels suffered heavy losses.

In 2002, the Government of India decided to disinvest in many public sector undertakings. ITDC was one of them. The rationale was that public sector as a whole, did not have a role in providing hospitality services in metro locations where the private sector had established adequate presence in the market. It was also felt that in non-metro and other locations where the private sector hotels were yet to establish a presence, the public sector may be better suited to play the role of a facilitator rather than direct provider of services.

Problems faced while disinvesting
Though there was a broad consensus across the political spectrum that government had no business to be in hotel industry, there was lot of resistance when actually the Disinvestment Ministry, which was created by the Indian government exclusively to disinvest/privatize the state-owned companies actually started the process of disinvesting ITDC hotels. The management and the bureaucracy at various levels tried to play the spoilt sport. There was

subtle resistance from civil servants to surrender their control. The magnitude of the task itself served as a major obstacle. Labor did not protest too much. The workers had reconciled to the fact that hotels will be privatized. They were worried about the delay in the process of privatization because it was hurting them the most.

There were other legal irritants. Most of the hotels under disinvestment did not have a title deed i.e. they had no clear ownership of the land on which the hotels were built. In addition, those hotels, which were on leasehold, land almost on a rent free basis. Most of the hotels had neither a completion certificate nor a fire safety certificate, which was mandatory for any private building.

The timing of the disinvestment of hotels came when the world tourism industry was at its lowest after the 9/11 incident in the US.

However, valuers were appointed to advise the government on value of each of the properties of ITDC. The hotels were demerged in smaller companies and most of the hotels were put on auction. Discounted cash flow method was used to value the property and government fixed a reserve price based on these valuations. They were sold as going concerns. The government decided to sell off all the hotels except the Ashok Hotel at New Delhi and Ashok Hotel at Bangalore which was leased to an establish chain of hotels on management contract. Only two hotels in Delhi are still standing, one is an office, and another is kept by the government for security reasons; the rest of the hotels were put on sale. A number of hotels were sold at throwaway prices.

There has been a lot of criticism about the modus operandi of the entire disinvestment of ITDC. In a lot of quarters, it has been felt that the government sold the properties for a song. In spite of all these criticisms, the government considers the ITDC disinvestment as a success story of privatization in India.

Today the government has an equity participation of 51 percent in ITDC and the corporation has 49 percent equity participation. ITDC's accommodation chain is the largest in the country. It offers accommodation ranging from luxury suites to modestly furnished rooms, from beach resorts to moderately priced forest lodges. This accounts for almost four thousand rooms all over India. For the government, the ITDC runs about hundred and twenty restaurants serving different cuisines.

Apart from this, ITDC, continues to have its transport network and its duty-free shops.

The change in the policy of the Government of India reflects the change in time world over. From a partially controlled and centrally planned economy, India is slowly emerging into the market economy. The role of the state is being re-defined based on the altered realities. This process is slow and tedious because India is an open society, and the largest functional democracy in the world.

Genpact - Generating Business Impact

Genpact began in 1997 as a business processing unit (called GE capital International services (GECIS) within General Electric. It started with the mandate to provide business process services to GE capital's businesses globally. This new unit inherited the parent company's deep understanding of process. The Lean and Six Sigma principles were applied to Business process operations. This helped them to obtain outstanding process efficiencies and operational effectiveness.

Within eight years, the company earned the opportunity to manage a wide range of processes across all of GE's financial services, in addition to their manufacturing businesses globally.

In January 2005, GECIS became Genpact. Genpact completed a successful IPO in August 2007 and got listed on the NYSE. From 2007–2010, Genpact became increasingly international. The process expertise and unique DNA in Lean Six Sigma was extended to other clients. The company made rapid strides and increased from nineteen thousand employees and annual revenues of USD 491.90 to sixty-eight thousand employees and annual revenues of USD 2.28 billion as of 2014. Bain capital became Genpact's largest shareholder in Nov 2012, with the strategic objective to grow the company further. The focus was on definition of their solution portfolio, improvement of client relationship in the front end as well as a deepening of domain expertise and related bench of subject matter experts.

In spite of Genpact's success, analysts have basic questions on future client retention. "BPO only services have a strong value proposition for the first three to five years of an engagement driven by arbitrage and operational efficiencies and effectiveness. Genpact has been successful in riding this wave," says Saurabh Gupta, of the Everest Group. But once you're done with that phase, a BPO has to come up with a bagful of tricks that can demonstrate to clients that there is still a lot to be gained in employing the firm.

During April to June 2011, quite a few surprises emanated from the Genpact stable. It announced the acquisition of Headstrong Corporation, Virginia based IT consulting and services player with a strong presence in capital markets and healthcare for USD 550 million. In May, Pramod Bhasin, who steered the company successfully for thirteen years, stepped aside into a non-executive role of vice-chairman.

These developments marked a significant change in the basic character of Genpact. From being a pure BPO, it had to embrace a different business model.

Why did this happen to Genpact? The changing dynamic of the IT sector had a role to play in this. For a most part, there were pure-play IT companies and then there were pure-play BPO companies. Initially most companies worked with multiple vendors. Gradually, however, most companies started demanding end-to-end solutions from their vendors. One, it was easy to deal with lesser number of vendors and secondly, a known vendor would know the processes well.

To satisfy the changing demands of the customer, ITeS companies started acquiring BPOs one after another. Genpact, then GECIS was able to hold its own in this environment. Being strong in process management, they were able to spread their wings to manufacturing, capital markets, banking, legal services, insurance, consumer goods, transportation, and business service sectors providing HR and legal services, procurement and supply chain, collections and customer service. Being part of a large conglomerate such as GE helped the company.

However, Genpact's golden run was affected by the economic slowdown in the aftermath of the financial breakdown in 2008. Squeezing margins, shrinking size of contracts, shorter deal cycles and rising competition with ITeS players was making the climate difficult for pure play BPOs. In keeping with the requirements of the hour, Genpact just decided to do things better and more efficiently and become a complete solutions provider.

The Headstrong acquisition happened against this backdrop. It signaled Genpact's ambition to aggressively grow its Consulting and IT Services pie in tandem with its business process management business. The Jawood (healthcare) acquisition helped to bring IT expertise in terms of new *BPO platforms*. Also with that came a new group of clients in the fastest growing segments in the BPO space. On the other hand, it was slowly depending less and less on GE. Today GE's contribution to Genpact's revenues is about 19 percent (down from 100 percent in 2004). Today, Genpact manages more than 4500 processes, which it has re-engineered for six hundred clients many of who are top notch companies like Astra Zeneca, Cadbury, Schweppes, GlaxoSmithKline, Beecham to name a few.

Over the past few years, Genpact has slowly geared itself for the *integrated play*. After seeing IT vendors like TCS, Infosys, Capgemini, HCL, IBM, Accenture, etc. aggressively cross sell their BPM capabilities to their clients who earlier bought IT services from them, Genpact had made six other acquisitions, besides Headstrong in a twenty-four month timeframe.

BPO businesses depend heavily on the quality of their resources. Genpact adopted a very people friendly approach. Various initiatives were employed to keep the people engaged.

- Genpact followed global best practices to ensure that its employees stay engaged and retained them by giving them fruitful and rewarding careers. Due to this, in 2009, the company had a very low attrition rate of 22 percent—the lowest in the industry. For the year 2014, the attrition rate has been 25 percent. This has been recognized by prestigious organizations like Global Services Media, COPC (Customer operations Productivity Center) and Frost and Sullivan.
- **Hiring:** Genpact brought in employees in numerous ways—employee referrals, storefronts, online applications, campus recruitments, and headhunters.
- **Training:** Genpact believes in training and places huge focus there. Employees had to be trained on various fronts—Process Training, Voice and Accent Training, Lean and Sigma training, Culture Training etc.

They believed that training was critical for success.

- **Talent Retention:** Genpact laid a lot of emphasis on this and developed a holistic approach to meeting employee needs.
- **Leadership Development:** A key learning that Genpact learned early from its GE days was the importance of developing top talent into future leaders of Genpact. They believed that organizations that identify, promote, and develop their leaders from within are better placed than their peers.
- They developed leadership programs that were designed to broaden leadership skills and business acumen. These **BUILD** programs were focused on developing middle managers for leadership roles through an eighteen month structured program. These programs were important as they created the leadership pool.
- **Rewards and Recognition:** Performance management is a critical area for Genpact and they spend a lot of effort in planning each employee's career and aligning their goals with larger organizational goals. When every goal an employee is appraised on is linked to a bigger organizational goal, accountability and ownership is driven on the job every single day.

- **Communication and Engagement:** Genpact uses multiple channels like town halls, web chats, the intranet, one-on-one meetings, etc., to regularly connect and communicate with employees. Another key channel of taking feedback is the Employee Satisfaction Survey. T, the results of which are driven with rigor and passion throughout the company.
- **Measuring and Preventing Attrition** - In its early days, Genpact experienced attrition amongst associates who were leaving to pursue higher education. Therefore, they decided to offer them the chance to study while continuing to work at Genpact. They started the Education@work initiative. Partnering with Premier B schools like IIMs. NMIMS, XLRI, IMT and other prominent educational bodies, the company offers employees courses to develop their career skills while working with the firm.
- **Special Focus on Gender Diversity** - Genpact has come a long way in realizing the importance of a diverse workforce from a gender standpoint. The drive also came from customers who demanded that they include more women at the leadership level. It is an internal mandate to bring gender diversity at the top level to 25 percent. To achieve this, there are a lot of initiatives taken to hire, train, and retain women employees.

In the past few years, Genpact has been underperforming. This is uncharacteristic because the company has a superb record of delivery and a history of great performance. The changing market scenario has caused it to lose its sweet spot. But the company has also been doing many right things. The finance and accounting BPO practice has been at the heart of its growth engine. In the recent past, there have been fewer F&A deals of that size coming in the market as the market has matured. The direct competition for Genpact has been Accenture and IBM who are also masters in the F&A space.

The company has been adopting many strategies to counter this shifting market. The headquarters of Genpact shifted to the United States. Tiger Tyagarajan, a world class sales and marketing executive, took over as CEO. The company worked very hard to set up new lines of business.

While presenting the outlook for 2015, what Tiger Tyagarajan said sums it all. "There is a disruptive trend sweeping across industries requiring companies to integrate new technology and find new ways to use data and insights as a competitive advantage. Our strategy is focused on building domain led solutions that are responsive to this trend. We believe we are on the right path to further differentiate Genpact and increase our competitiveness and are excited by the momentum in our business."

Infosys

On June 1 2013, Mr. NR Narayanamurthy, one of the founders of Infosys, returned to the company as Executive Chairman and Additional Director. Seven years after he stepped out of Infosys, he was back in an executive capacity. His appointment came after the company's performance slipped over the last two years. Its growth was lower than industry growth. The idea of bringing Murthy back was to set the company back on its wheels.

After Murthy's arrival, the company won two hundred and thirty eight clients and its revenue growth doubled to 11.5 percent. The stock gained over 20 percent, being the highest gain in a year.

There was a dearth of leaders from within the company. The company was on the lookout for someone from outside, but it did not materialize and Murthy came back into the helm.

Infosys was the product of one man's vision. N R Narayanamurthy, as an employee of Patni computers Ltd. in Pune, saw the enormous price difference between the pay for software engineering in India versus that in overseas markets like the United States.

Infosys was set up in 1981 with a capital of INR 10,000. In 1993, the company went public and the stock was offered at INR 95. In 1998, after several 1:1 bonuses, the share price of Infosys was around INR 2610. Initial investors had multiplied their investment capital nearly eighty times in five years while Infosys had grown to become a leading player in the software services industry.

From the very beginning, Infosys founders were *born global*. The company focused on the most competitive market. The first clients were U.S. based. This clearly showed the global focus rather than taking the route of establishing themselves in India first. The founders realized early on that significant growth could be achieved by having an international presence. This was important to gain an international reputation.

Another founding principle was to be a *globally respected corporation*. The company culture instills not only compliance-driven but also a values-driven corporate behavior. This meant that they would have to adhere to local regulations and international standards and guidelines, while all the time delivering value to their stakeholders. Infosys summarizes its values system as **C-LIFE** i.e. Client Value, Leadership by example, Integrity and transparency, Fairness and Excellence

They believed in investing in human capital, which is recruiting and retaining the best available talent worldwide.

Fourthly, Infosys relied extensively on strategic partnerships for co-creation and co-evolution. Co-creation was engaging partners and clients in the creation of intellectually driven business solutions. Co-evolution was working with clients closely to project future trends and challenges, developing solutions that help the clients and also help the company adapt.

These guiding principles (named Infosys 1.0) pioneered the company's Global Delivery Model. It created an offshore software development center in Bangalore. When the work was brought back from the client's site, it helped to both scale and skill. Cost was kept low. This also allowed for increased productivity through the 24 hour operations. Scope of project and delivery dates were assessed by people travelling from India to the client site and assessing the work on hand. This team which did the assessment, returned to India to do the software development. After completion, part of the team would go back for implementation of the software at the clients' site. Due to a lot of knowledge transfer that such a business process required, a high level of process discipline was required.

Also as part of this exercise, Infosys set up a marketing office in the US and offices in London and around Europe. Most of Infosys' customers were located overseas and activities such as marketing and customer service were carried out in the country of the customer. In this phase, the company was internally focused on building infrastructure and developing its skill base. Various support functions were created to aid operations. Training of employees took center stage.

By 1998, Infosys had grown from the original seven to over three thousand people.

The company achieved two very demanding benchmarks in the arena of software quality standards—ISO 9001 and SEI CMM level 4. With these certifications, the company signaled powerfully to the market that Infosys was positioning itself as a high quality player in the global software development space, competing with the best in technical and managerial competency.

In 1998, officials from the New York Stock Exchange NASDAQ visited India scouting for listing prospects. Patrick Sutch, NASDAQ, Asia Pacific Head said that Infosys "is an American Company in India." That embodies the inherent nature of the company. The company had an Indian heart but was very American in its aspects of operation.

According to Narayanamurthy, the success of Infosys was due to its ability to attract, develop, and retain outstanding human capital. They could only compete on the basis of their people. Therefore, employees had to be experts both in technical knowledge and domains related to the customer's business.

Attrition rates were low in the company. It is believed that the personal charisma of Narayanamurthy helped retain people in the company. However, beyond this, Infosys had pioneered a system, which ensured that employees had a full share of the fortunes of the firm. Infosys had pioneered employee stock options. These stock options made many employees millionaires many times over. The company did not give stock options to companies less than market rate. To avoid regulatory barriers, a special trust was created at the time of going public and they allocated a large part of its equity to this trust at the original issue price. From this pool, stock options were given to the employees. This proved to be a masterstroke to attract and retain talent.

In spite of this, the company did face a lot of pressure on three fronts—commoditization, cost, and competition. Software industry was facing a lot of threat from commoditization of the business. Small operators were threatening the company with competitive pricing. In India, salaries constituted 30 percent of the revenue of the software companies. At that time, the salaries were rising at about 25 percent annually and costs were going up 7.5 percent every year. Therefore, the company's margins were declining. The intense competition was also a critical factor. Nilekani said, "the industry as a whole is teaching the customers how to negotiate. It is destroying itself."

The strategy of globalization was Infosys' response to the pressures. The only way to protect and enhance margins was to move up the value curve.

While during Infosys 1.0, the company spent a lot of resources in developing its people, Sanjay Purohit, the then Senior Vice president and global head of Products, platforms and solutions says, "The first 15 years were about setting the base, laying down the founding stones. The next 15 years—Infosys 2.0—saw the model being proven and developed very good traction as we grew."

During Infosys 2.0, the company identified four axes to drive its expansion. The first lay in expanding into other industries. It invested in building industry knowledge.

The second route forward was to expand the suite of services it offered. In its first incarnation, Infosys was essentially an application development and maintenance company. Then it started the suite of services it offered to include enterprise solutions, infrastructure management, testing, as well as business process outsourcing. "Suddenly we were operating in multiple industries with both industry specific and bespoke solutions. So that was a genetic transition of the company from being services-oriented to being solutions-oriented," says Purohit.

The third important axis was geography. Initially, Infosys' global view led to it becoming US centric so that, at one point, almost 75 percent of its revenues came from the U.S. It then expanded into Europe starting with the UK, and then subsequently into Switzerland, Germany, France, and then Eastern Europe.

It also expanded into the South and Latin American markets, Australia, Japan, and China. By the end of 2012, Infosys had a five-thousand person strong development center and its own campus in China.

The fourth focus was on clients. Astonishingly, 95 to 97 percent of Infosys' business comes from repeat clients. It identified a group of clients that it wanted to work with in order to build credibility and then went after them.

After a relatively quiet start, Infosys' growth accelerated. For Infosys, growth is seen as constant proof of its credibility. B. G. Srinivas, who was heading Infosys in Europe at that time, comments on the company's approach to growth. "We have always built a culture that's emphasized not getting bogged down by constraints, but looking at ways of driving ambitious growth plans. Behind that is the core of what we build on—our core values and ethics. We have robust internal processes, which help sustain growth. If you look at our vision, it says we want to be a globally respected corporation. We are not saying we want to be the biggest."

Infosys 3.0 was launched in 2011, and was geared toward making the company much more client focused along three dimensions: Value, Relevancy, and Strategic Partnerships. At the heart of this initiative was a strategic framework called *Building Tomorrow's Enterprise* (BTE). The framework identifies seven themes, which Infosys perceived as being key to delivering client value for the emerging future "Our strategy is to make ourselves relevant. We've seen how we bring consulting led transformation capabilities to our clients, how we bring technology driven optimization and how we bring innovation," says Purohit. Transform, Innovate, Optimize is the mantra.

Moreover, the strategy was to have a balanced portfolio across business segments as well as geographically. The company aimed to achieve a significant portion of future revenues from the products and platforms space, co-creating value for clients based on intellectual property driven solutions, thus differentiating itself further from the traditional application development and maintenance segment which was becoming more competitive and commoditized.

However, while all these developments were taking place at the business end, the company saw its fair share of changes at the top. In 2011–12, Narayanamurthy exited Infosys. He served as CEO from 1981 to 2002 and as chairman from 2002 to 2011. In 2011, he stepped down from the board and became chairman emeritus. On June 1, 2013, Murthy was appointed as Additional Director and Executive Chairman for a period of five years. On June 12, 2014, it was announced that Murthy would step down as executive chairman. Later in October that year, he was designated chairman emeritus.

He was succeeded by Nandan Nilekani. Nilekani became CEO in March 2002 and served as CEO of the company through April 2007 when he relinquished his position to Kris Gopalakrishnan and became co-chairman of the board of directors. Nilekani left Infosys in 2009 to join the government in its new initiative as chairman of Unique Identification Authority of India.

Kris Gopalakrishnan became CEO and MD of Infosys in 2007 and later became president and Joint MD from Aug 2006. His responsibilities included customer services, technology, investments, and acquisitions. In Aug 2011, he handed over this responsibility of CEO and MD to another co-founder, S D Shibulal. He was later appointed Exec Vice chairman of Infosys Board. He went on to serve as non-exec vice chairman of Infosys board until Oct 2014.

Apart from this crisis of leadership, the company's revenues faltered. On 13 April 2013, after its earnings announcement, the Infosys scrip had fallen by 21 percent, its worst decline in a decade. This event had spooked several insiders, including the board members. Narayanamurthy was invited by the board members to take up the mantle of chairman once again. He was hesitant at first, but later decided to come back on board. The board passed a unanimous resolution appointing Murthy as chairman. During this stint, he insisted that his son Rohan Murthy would assist him as his executive assistant. Both only wanted a notional compensation of Re. 1 per year for their services. Murthy also said that his son would not have any leadership role in Infosys.

At the time of taking over, Narayanamurthy stressed the importance of winning more technology contracts that focus on application development as well as remote infrastructure management, two areas that Infosys during the past two years have termed commoditized and low margin. These are also the areas where rivals have been overtaking Infosys and scoring on the growth front.

However, the quest for CEO continued. In a major break from tradition, Infosys brought in an outsider as

CEO, breaking the tradition of keeping the job amongst the co-founders.

The decision to appoint Dr. Vishal Sikka was intensely debated within the company, which had seen a spate of top-level exits the past few months. However, the nominations committee, after meeting several candidates, shortlisted four and finally zeroed in on Sikka. He took over as CEO and Managing Director in August 2014.

The first non-promoter CEO Vishal Sikka experiment failed miserably and saw the unceremonious exit of this high profile leader.

The new CEO, also a non-promoter, is Salil Parekh. It seems to be a more low-key affair. One needs to wait and watch how Infosys turns around under his leadership.

APPENDIX II

Employee Engagement Survey

We conducted a very different kind of an employee engagement survey, because I strongly believe that a global model like Gallup's Q12 cannot be used as is.

Here are findings of the mini-survey along with the engagement questions we asked. I believe these questions throw up far more important pointers than a "one fit for all" engagement survey:

Sample

Eighty-three participants from nineteen companies across India took this survey. They came from the following companies:

- Amazon.com
- Astra Zeneca

- Banca Sella
- CGI
- Columbia Asia Hospital
- CTS
- HP India
- Mindtree
- Omega Healthcare
- Oracle SSI
- Philips Electronics
- Philips Intellectual Property Systems
- Pace
- Subex
- TCS
- The Himalaya Drug Company
- The Chancery Pavilion
- TP Vision India
- Yokogawa

The distribution of participants by industry is given in the table below. The designations of the participants are from middle to senior management, in the following roles.

- Program Manager / Senior Program Manager
- Project Director
- Technical Head
- Service Delivery Manager / Service Delivery Head

Industry	No. of participants
Information Technology	44
Services	14
Manufacturing	13
Marketing	8
Banking and Financial Services	4

Method

- A battery of attitude statements were given and participants were asked to select their most appropriate rating for each of the statements
- In most cases, A simple 5-point 'Agree-Disagree' scale used to obtain responses

    Completely Agree   5
    Somewhat agree   4
    Neither agree nor disagree   3
    Somewhat disagree   2
    Completely disagree   1

- In a few cases, where a 5-point scale was seen to not yield accurate responses, a dichotomous scale (e.g. Agree / Disagree) was used
- At the end of the survey, participants were provided opportunity to render additional comments

Results

- Only 15 percent of employees Completely Agreed that they were part of a family (Statement: *We are like one family.*)
- Nearly 54 percent of employees Completely Agreed that their contribution was valued (Statement: *My contribution is valued.*)
- Nearly 75 percent of employees opined that their career and growth opportunities discussed periodically (Statement: *Career and growth opportunities are discussed periodically.*)
- 44 percent felt that they did not have to suck up to their manager or boss to get promoted or recognized (Statement: *I don't have to suck up to my manager or boss to get promoted or recognized.*)
- 51 percent of employees opined that they would think twice before changing their job even if their salary was more (Statement: *I will think twice before changing my job even if the salary was more.*)
- As regards managers and the relationship maintained with families of employees, scores were low indicating that perhaps there was indeed something missing, only 30 percent of the participants completely agreed that their manager knew their family members

(Statement: *My manager knows my family members.*)

- Only 25 percent of them completely agreed that their manager attended the family functions. (Statement: *My manager will attend important family functions.*)
- Only a third of the employees completely agreed that their exit family was as warm and friendly as their entry policy. Interestingly, an equal number remained neutral in their responses.

APPENDIX II B

Performance Appraisal Survey

Sample

Hundred and five participants from twenty-two companies across India took this survey. They came from the following companies:

- Astra Zeneca
- Banca Sella
- CGI
- Columbia Asia Hospital
- CTS
- HP India
- JPMorgan Chase
- Mindtree
- Oracle
- Omega Healthcare
- Oracle SSI

- Philips Electronics
- Philips Intellectual Property Systems
- Pace
- RBS
- Rulesware LLC
- Subex
- The Himalaya Drug Company
- The Park Bangalore
- TP Vision India
- USL
- Yokogawa

The distribution of participants by industry is given in the table below. The designations of the participants are from middle to senior management, in the following roles.

- Program manager / Senior Program Manager / Competency manager / Principal Consultant
- Project Director / VP & MD /
- Technical Head / Software Architect / Expert Technologist
- QA Manager / Delivery Manager

Industry	No. of participants
Information Technology	64
Services	16
Manufacturing	15
Marketing	5
Banking and Financial Services	5

Method

- A battery of attitude statements were given and participants were asked to select their most appropriate rating for each of the statements
- In most cases, A simple 5-point "Agree-Disagree" scale used to obtain responses

    Completely Agree   5
    Somewhat agree   4
    Neither agree nor disagree 3
    Somewhat disagree   2
    Completely disagree   1

- In a few cases where a 5-point scale was seen to not yield accurate responses, a dichotomous scale (e.g., Agree / Disagree) was used
- At the end of the survey, participants were provided opportunity to render additional comments

Findings

- Only 49 percent were in complete agreement with their appraisal system
- Only a third of HR employees felt that the rating system was transparent and objective
- Only 46 percent of participants expressed agreement that their manager reviewed their performance on a regular basis while close to 30 percent was in disagreement with this and the remaining took a neutral stand.
- Only 39 percent of the participants felt that there were no surprises in their appraisal
- Only 48 percent of participants completely agreed that their rating system was fair and clear while nearly 20 percent completely disagreed to it and nearly 30 percent assumed neutral stance.
- While 44 percent of employees felt that their appraisal system helped them to improve and grow, 22 percent completely disagreed to it.
- 21 percent of employees agreed that the process for selection, promotion, and recognition was transparent and based solely on merit while 52 percent completely disagreed to it.
- Nearly 75 percent stated that caste or creed did not play a role in selection, promotion and recognition practices in the organization.

References

Ghoshal, Sumantra; Piramal Gita; Budhiraja, Sudeep. (2001) World Class in India – A Casebook of Companies in Transformation. Penguin India

http://www.livemint.com/Opinion/BxhKMMvIA7tPjzoyQRLMHP/Dj-View--Why-did-HMT-fail.html

http://timesofindia.indiatimes.com/city/bengaluru/HMT-caught-in-a-time-warp/articleshow/42557940.cms

http://www.deccanchronicle.com/141002/nation-current-affairs/article/hmt-winds-watch-still-collector%E2%80%99s-delight

http://blogs.reuters.com/india/2014/09/19/fans-rush-to-hmt-as-watchmaker-marks-time/

http://www.business-standard.com/article/beyond-business/the-story-of-taj-111121700080_1.html

http://archive.indianexpress.com/news/tata-launches-book-on-history-of-taj-hotel/888992/

http://www.tata.co.in/company/profile/Indian-Hotels

http://www.tata.co.in/company/articlesinside/tHf!$$$!0f6sFuE=/TLYVr3YPkMU=

http://www.tajhotels.com/about-taj/company-information/default.html

http://www.gingerhotels.com/about-us

http://www.tata.com/company/articlesinside/Leg-up-for-employment

http://www.business-standard.com/article/companies/tata-realty-and-infra-to-foray-into-hospitality-112050600013_1.html

http://www.tata.in/article/inside/qGSY!$$$$!cWnN88=/TLYVr3YPkMU=

http://www.tajhotels.com/about-taj/careers/taj-values.html

http://www.rediff.com/money/special/spcc-indian-hotels-four-brand-strategy-for-success/20101011.htm

https://nitawriter.wordpress.com/2006/11/24/the-story-of-one-of-the-brand-taj/

http://www.travelclick.com/en/news-events/press-release/taj-hotels-resorts-and-palaces-takes-business-intelligence-enterprise-level-travelclick%E2%80%99s

http://www.indiaincorporated.com/item/3234-tata-ethos-imperative-to-success-india-inc-interview.html

http://www.forbes.com/sites/kevinkruse/2012/10/08/employee-recognition/

http://www.tata.in/article/inside/Kqb!$$$!Jbwztco=/TLYVr3YPkMU=

http://www.ukessays.com/essays/tourism/a-detailed-breakdown-of-taj-hotel-tourism-essay.php

http://www.theashokgroup.com/index.php?option=com_content&view=article&id=3&lang=en

http://archive.indianexpress.com/news/from-a-speck-of-dust...the-allnew-delhi-story/730879/

http://shodhganga.inflibnet.ac.in/bitstream/10603/22675/8/08_chapter%202.pdf

http://www.thehindubusinessline.com/markets/stock-markets/cabinet-panel-approves-stake-sale-in-stc-itdc/article4905606.ece

http://economictimes.indiatimes.com/india-tourism-development-corporation-ltd/infocompanyhistory/companyid-4594.cms

http://www.hospitalitybizindia.com/detailNews.aspx?aid=15459&sid=6

http://economictimes.indiatimes.com/india-tourism-development-corporation-ltd/infocompanyhistory/companyid-4594.cms

http://en.wikipedia.org/wiki/India_Tourism_Development_Corporation

http://ashwanilohani.blogspot.in/2013/10/why-sell-family-silver.html

http://scholarworks.umass.edu/cgi/viewcontent.cgi?article=1044&context=jhfm

http://www.csstc.org/reports/egm/P4/Presentation_India.htm (privatization of state owned enterprises)

video lecture of ITDC
http://www.learnerstv.com/video/Free-video-Lecture-18472-Management.htm

http://www.mbaskool.com/brandguide/tourism-and-hospitality/2894-ashok-group.html

http://www.divest.nic.in/RFP%20of%20ITDC.pdf

https://books.google.co.in/books?id=6C59BAAAQBAJ&pg=PA276&lpg=PA276&dq=case+studies+of+ITDC&source=bl&ots=QX_TxPAoyi&sig=-fLj8Zuz_ekNCR7wIbGwD5FDE7Y&hl=en&sa=X&ei=Idf-VLLJNs2MuAStuYGwDg&ved=0CE4Q6AEwBw#v=onepage&q=case%20studies%20of%20ITDC&f=false

http://indiatoday.intoday.in/story/sale-of-itdc-hotels-unearth-sordid-tales-of-abuse-of-power-loot-and-corruption/1/219434.html

http://www.iimb.ernet.in/research/sites/default/files/Reflections%20on%20India's%20tourism%20policy.pdf

http://www.divest.nic.in/chap16.asp

http://www.genpact.com/home/about-us/company-overview

http://www.genpact.com/docs/default-source/pdf/driving-competitive-advantage-in-uncertain-times

http://www.businessworld.in/news/economy/genpact-at-crossroads/384853/page-1.html

http://www.peoplematters.in/article/2009/09/01/c-suite/genpact-leading-through-uncertain-times/124

http://www.business-standard.com/article/companies/can-genpact-fend-off-it-services-challenge-113031300014_1.html

http://www.everestgrp.com/2014-03-genpacts-q4-performance-a-cautionary-tale-for-all-service-providers-sherpas-in-blue-shirts-13423.html

http://www.moneycontrol.com/news-topic/genpact/

http://info.shine.com/tag/genpact.html

http://www.business-standard.com/article/companies/genpact-profit-drops-11-6-revenue-up-11-2-115050200027_1.html

http://investors.genpact.com/phoenix.zhtml?c=209334&p=irol-newsArticle&ID=2058078

http://investors.genpact.com/phoenix.zhtml?c=209334&p=irol-news&nyo=0

http://www.moneycontrol.com/news/features/nse-fin-wiz-visits-genpact_1337624.html

http://investors.genpact.com/phoenix.zhtml?c=209334&p=irol-newsArticle&ID=2013682

www.infosys.com

Wikipedia

http://articles.economictimes.indiatimes.com/2014-06-05/news/50359146_1_bg-srinivas-ceo-shibulal-infy/2

http://businesstoday.intoday.in/story/narayana-murthy-returns-to-infosys-rescue/1/195494.html

http://forbesindia.com/blog/business-strategy/why-did-narayana-murthy-come-back-to-infosys/

http://en.wikipedia.org/wiki/N._R._Narayana_Murthy

https://books.google.co.in/books?id=bX1y00gj6wMC&pg=PA291&lpg=PA291&dq=infosys+journey+in+the+last+decade&source=bl&ots=yEfrj11D8M&sig=M3LiFlHQglf3kre5t3xKvqldGJg&hl=en&sa=X&ei=wKwoVY3GOpGVuASa3YC4Bg&ved=0CEQQ6AEwBw#v=onepage&q=infosys%20journey%20in%20the%20last%20decade&f=false

http://www.sciencedirect.com/science/article/pii/S0970389614000871#bib2

http://www.sciencedirect.com/science/article/pii/S0970389614000871

http://www.london.edu/faculty-and-research/lbsr/what-next-for-infosys#.VTyhFtKqqko

http://economictimes.indiatimes.com/tech/ites/nr-narayana-murthy-back-as-executive-chairman-is-this-what-infosys-needed/articleshow/20387396.cms

http://www.livemint.com/Companies/1fFlFdRFtVSY3E3GJTQhAK/Infosys-brings-back-N-R-Narayana-Murthy-as-exective-chairm.html

http://www.livemint.com/Companies/beFc2rmqEpgybNaVcyzkyH/What-went-down-at-Infosys.html

http://economictimes.indiatimes.com/tech/ites/nr-narayana-murthy-back-as-executive-chairman-is-this-what-infosys-needed/articleshow/20387396.cms

http://www.thehindubusinessline.com/companies/rohan-was-brought-in-to-bring-fresh-new-perspectives-murthy/article6115143.ece

http://www.thehindubusinessline.com/companies/vishal-sikka-is-new-infosys-ceo/article6106530.ece

A Request

Thank You for Reading My Book!

I really appreciate all of your feedback, and I love hearing what you have to say.

I need your input to make the next version of this book and my future books even better.

Please leave me a helpful review on Amazon letting me know what you think of the book.

Thank you so much!
~ Naresh Purushotham
<u>npurushotham@gmail.com</u>

www.ingramcontent.com/pod-product-compliance
Lightning Source LLC
Chambersburg PA
CBHW031611210526
45464CB00004B/1527